EXPERIENCES OF THE SEX INDUSTRY

Natasha Mulvihill

I0136016

BRISTOL
UNIVERSITY
PRESS

First published in Great Britain in 2024 by

Bristol University Press
University of Bristol
1-9 Old Park Hill
Bristol
BS2 8BB
UK
t: +44 (0)117 374 6645
e: bup-info@bristol.ac.uk

Details of international sales and distribution partners are available at bristoluniversitypress.co.uk

© Bristol University Press 2024

British Library Cataloguing in Publication Data
A catalogue record for this book is available from the British Library

ISBN 978-1-5292-1655-4 hardcover
ISBN 978-1-5292-1656-1 paperback
ISBN 978-1-5292-1657-8 ePub
ISBN 978-1-5292-1658-5 ePdf

Cover design: Dave Worth
Front cover image: gettyimages/R. Tsubin

With thanks to the research participants.
All views in this book are the author's own.

Contents

List of Figures and Tables

Figure

Table

Introduction

Aims of the book

If you picked up this book thinking it was about sex, then you may be disappointed. This book is primarily about people and their stories. It emerged from a UK Home Office report that I and other colleagues at the University of Bristol[1] were commissioned to write on the 'nature and prevalence of prostitution and sex work in England and Wales'. As part of the research for that report, I conducted written email interviews with more than 40 individuals currently or formerly involved in the sex industry. Since that data could be used only sparingly, given the page constraints of the final report published in October 2019 (Hester et al, 2019), I asked our participants if I could write up their interviews in a book, and indeed re-interview them about their reflections on participating in the research and the impact of COVID-19, which arrived in early 2020. Their accounts provide the central substance and structure for this book. They describe how they became involved in the sex industry, their experiences and their plans for the future.

I have been researching the sex industry in England since the late 2000s, a journey first sparked by teaching creative writing to women exiting street work. Indeed, for the first few years of my research, the experiences of, and government policy related to, women involved in street sex working was my main focus. Academic research and feminist debates on the sex industry are hotly contested. Exchanging sex for money is seen variously as a career, as a survival strategy, as feminist, as anti-feminist, as violence against women, as an empowering challenge to expectations of passive female sexuality or as an outcome of patriarchy and other social power relations. 'So, it is across the bodies of sex workers that feminist debates play out' (Sanders et al, 2017, p 5). Researching in this area can be difficult and over the years I have picked my way through the debates, seeing value in arguments on both sides, but limitations too. As a researcher in the Centre for Gender and Violence, that has perhaps made my research a somewhat awkward fit. Unlike the unequivocal harms of rape or domestic abuse, while parts of the sex industry fit the gendered violence template, significant areas fall outside too.

For me personally, the Home Office work provided an intellectual catalyst to listen to those currently involved in selling and buying sex and to try and articulate that complexity to policymakers. It enabled us as a research team to gain insight into the experiences of hundreds of those involved in the sex industry, who responded to our online survey and to questionnaires distributed through charities and projects and some completed by hand. However, it also presented another dilemma. Sex workers, as well as those in chaotic and constrained situations engaging in survival sex, are a highly scrutinized and repeatedly researched group. And the value of this repeated research is not always clear. In England and Wales in 2019 alone, the Conservative Party, the Work and Pensions Committee, the Women and Equalities Committee and the Home Office launched or reported inquiries into the sex industry. Likely some of the same individuals contributed. Yet there has been no policy change. And so, as academics, we can be complicit in trawling the seabed of people's lives, opening up emotions and memories, without the power to provide any material or structural restoration.

Policy context

The approach to prostitution in England and Wales[2] in previous decades has been a mix of de facto tolerance for transactions which take place out of sight, combined with periodic strong policing of outdoor sex work or brothel-keeping. This distinction between the public and private sphere follows the 1957 Wolfenden Committee Report which asserted that 'there must remain a sphere of private morality and immorality which is, in brief and crude terms, not the law's business' (Report of the Committee on Homosexual Offences and Prostitution, 1957, para 60). For this reason, a raft of legislation prohibits in England and Wales the 'public face' of sex work: loitering or soliciting for prostitution (Section 1 of the Street Offences Act 1959); kerb crawling (Section 51A of the Sexual Offences Act 2003); keeping a brothel (Sections 33–36 of the Sexual Offences Act 1956); or placing adverts in a public telephone box (Section 46(1) of the Criminal Justice and Police Act 2001).

The act of buying and selling sex, in the absence of coercion (Section 53A of the Sexual Offences Act 2003) or third-party facilitation, control and profit-making (Section 52 Causing or Inciting Prostitution for Gain and Controlling Prostitution for Gain and Section 53 Sexual Offences Act 2003) is however legal. While legislation has been updated to remove problematic terms such as 'common prostitute' or to make offences gender neutral, the substantive aims of legislation in this area have remained consistent over the decades.

Emerging concern in the 1990s about the trafficking of women and children for the purpose of sexual exploitation has arguably problematized, although not yet fundamentally disrupted, the approach to sex work in England and Wales. The United Nations Protocol to Prevent, Suppress and Punish Trafficking in Persons, Especially Women and Children, adopted in 2000, engendered a renewed focus on 'tackling the demand' for paid sex. Spanger (2011) argues that the renewed focus on trafficking created a space in which discussion of criminalization of sex purchase became possible. This is illustrated in the emergence of the 'Nordic model', an approach which criminalizes the sex buyer but not the seller. Introduced in Sweden in 1999 and adapted in some neighbouring countries in the earlier 2000s, laws to criminalize sex buyers have been passed more recently in France, Ireland, Canada and Israel. In England and Wales, the Labour government undertook a review of sex buyer 'demand' (Home Office, 2008) and the Home Secretary Jacqui Smith proposed part-criminalization in a speech to the Labour Party conference in that same year (Watt, 2008). Eventually adopted into law as Section 14 of the Policing and Crime Act 2009, the final clause was a rather narrower strict liability offence, applicable where a buyer pays for sexual services in the context of an identifiable and coercive third party.

In 2014, the All-Party Parliamentary Group (APPG) on Prostitution and the Sex Trade published *Shifting the Burden: Inquiry to Assess the Operation of the Current Legal Settlement in Prostitution in England and Wales*. This report reflected on actions following the Home Office Review on *Tackling Demand* in 2008, specifically Section 14 of the Policing and Crime Act, which the Committee claimed had been 'ineffective' with a low level of prosecutions (All-Party Parliamentary Group on Prostitution and the Global Sex Trade, 2014, p 5). In 2016, the Home Affairs Committee published its first review into prostitution. Committee members were perhaps not prepared for the complexity and depth of feeling that the sex industry engenders: 'It was originally intended to be a short inquiry. However, the evidence made clear to us that the views on the legal approach to prostitution are strongly held and highly polarised' (Home Affairs Committee, 2016, Conclusion, para 1). The Committee were not persuaded from the evidence presented to them that a law criminalizing sex buyers would be effective in 'reducing, rather than simply displacing, demand for prostitution, or in helping the police to tackle the crime and exploitation associated with the sex industry' (Home Affairs Committee, 2016, Conclusion, para 12). Indeed, the Committee appeared to be caught somewhere in the middle, finding that no model 'appears to offer a complete solution', though perhaps 'elements from the different models ... could usefully be applied in England and Wales' (Home Affairs Committee, 2016, Conclusion, para 16). The Committee did however recommend that the law on soliciting and brothel-keeping be reviewed urgently – in other words to decriminalize sellers in on- and off-street contexts. In addition, the Committee called for a better evidence base from which policymakers could develop effective legislation in this area:

> We were dismayed to discover the poor quality of information available about the extent and nature of prostitution in England and Wales. Without a proper evidence base, the Government cannot make informed decisions about the effectiveness of current legislation and policies, and cannot target funding and support interventions effectively. (Paragraph 36) … We recommend that the Home Office commissions an in-depth research study to help develop a better understanding of the current extent and nature of prostitution in England and Wales, and to draw together and put in context any recent relevant research. (Home Affairs Committee, 2016, Conclusion, para 16)

And so, in early 2018, the Home Office issued a tender for a report into the 'nature and prevalence of prostitution in England and Wales', which was awarded to our team at the University of Bristol, led by Professor Marianne Hester. Working from May 2018 through to June 2019, our brief was to stick squarely to description and avoid policy discussion: a tricky ask since most participants in our research saw it as an opportunity to lobby for change. Difficult too because, as the 'Centre for Gender and Violence Research', some expected us to be advocating for, or at least highlighting only evidence in favour of, a Nordic model. However, we took a pragmatic and exploratory approach, widening the brief with the following working definition: 'Prostitution and/or sex work constitutes the provision of sexual or erotic acts or sexual intimacy in exchange for payment or other benefit or need' (Hester et al, 2019, p 2).

We tried to ensure the report was strongly populated with the voices of those actually involved, or formerly involved, in the sex industry in England and Wales and to encourage caution about what can realistically be known, or at least generalized, in terms of 'nature', but especially 'prevalence'. This is because the accuracy and representativeness of researching often hidden and stigmatized groups will be affected strongly by who participates and who speaks. This in turn can tend to favour either those with more agency and resources, or those who are spoken *for* by non-governmental organizations (NGOs) or who are in contact with health and welfare services. It can mean that many – including those with irregular or conditional migrant status, those who are trafficked, coerced or exploited, those who do not engage with social media, activism or peer group support, or who are simply apprehensive of engaging with state-funded, particularly Home Office-funded, research – will likely be missed or under-represented. In addition, the diversity of experiences and settings within the sex industry mean that both quantitative and qualitative studies tend to be selective, local and contextual, rendering wider extrapolation problematic. Police force data, for example, will record only a partial insight into reported or identified sex transactions in a given geographical area.

Our final report offered evidence that the simple policy heuristic of 'forced' versus 'free' prostitution does not always map easily onto real lives and that many of the harms of the sex industry arise from social and economic factors, discrimination and inequality, criminalization and marginality. Perhaps the awkwardly complex and cross-governmental implications of what we found – from Universal Credit to student funding to disability to healthcare and beyond – delayed its publication through the summer of 2019. But finally, on 30 October 2019, as Britain woke to the news of a December general election, our report went live online, without an accompanying ministerial statement.

In January 2020, first reports emerged of a deadly virus in Wuhan in China, and for the next 18 months, much of the UK government policy agenda – sex work included – has been substantively focused on the COVID-19 pandemic. The work of collectives and NGOs such as the English Collective of Prostitutes, Sex Worker Rights Advocacy and Resistance Movement (SWARM), National Ugly Mugs (NUM), Beyond the Streets, Changing Lives and One25 has continued, particularly as the health crisis became a social and economic crisis for many, including those who sell sex.

This is the context in which this book emerges. Its purpose is to bring more fully into the light those original participant narratives. Quite deliberately, my commentary on these narratives is summarizing and observational rather than polemic, or especially academic. I was also interested in asking participants about their experience of being part of research and policy inquiries and to understand what happened for them next, once the report was published, the project closed, and government attention had moved elsewhere.

Existing literature

When I first began researching the sex industry in the late 2000s, I bought two books: *The Idea of Prostitution* (1997) by Sheila Jeffreys and *Sex Work: Writings by Women in the Sex Industry* (2001) edited by Frederique Delacoste and Priscilla Alexander. Jeffreys writes in the radical feminist tradition, identifying prostitution and 'prostituted women' as a form of sexual slavery and male domination (see similarly Barry, 1984). For Jeffreys, questions of individual agency or choice are irrelevant since all women are shaped and coerced by the forces of patriarchy. She therefore understands the exchange of sex for money as inherently exploitative. Delacoste and Alexander drew on (and further popularized) the 'sex as work' perspective, where prostitution is understood as labour, requiring attendant rights and protections. Their book is an edited collection of narratives written by sex workers themselves, who express both light and shade in assessing their work and their clients. Without realizing, I had bought two books which reflected the contested landscape of 'prostitution and sex work'.

In recent years, many more collections and anthologies by and about sex workers have emerged. These include a trilogy, *Prose and Lore: Memoir Stories and Sex Work* (Herman et al, 2014), published by The Red Umbrella Project; *Ho's Hookers, Call Girls and Rent Boys: Professional Writing on Life, Love, Money and Sex* (Sterry and Martin, 2009); *Johns, Marks, Tricks and Chickenhawks: Professionals & Their Clients Writing about Each Other* (Sterry and Martin, 2013); and *A Whore's Manifesto: An Anthology of Writing and Artwork by Sex Workers* (Kassirer, 2019). There has also been a resurgence of sex worker or sexual exploitation memoirs (see Kenney, 2012: examples include, Gee, 2011; O'Kelly, 2012; Mazzei, 2019), which reflects a wider trend of 'true confession' style biographies, perhaps catalysed by the success of Brooke Magnanti's ('Belle de Jour') *The Intimate Adventures of a London Call Girl*, published in 2007. Other writers and collections foreground experiences of exploitation and abuse in the sex trade, including Rachel Moran's *Paid For: My Journey Through Prostitution* (2015); Melinda Tankard Reist and Caroline Norma's 2016 collection *Prostitution Narratives: Stories of Survival in Sex Trade* and *An Untold Story: Experiences of Life and Street Prostitution in Hull* published by the Hull Lighthouse Project in 2017. Academics in the UK and Ireland (O'Neill, 1996; Phoenix, 1999; Sanders, 2008) and in North America (notably Dewey, 2011a, 2011b; Capous-Desyllas, 2013, 2014; Orchard et al, 2016; Dewey et al, 2018), have also used narrative, and sometimes visual, techniques to foreground the voices of those involved. Indeed, around the world, researchers have used art and stories to document sex worker experiences (see, for example, Oliveira, 2016; Carrier-Moisan, 2020). A focus on narrative is consistent with feminist research, since it starts with valuing 'women's perspectives and experiences' (Presser, 2005: 2067; see also Personal Narratives Group, 1989).

There are a small number of academic books written by current or former sex workers (for example, *Revolting Prostitutes: The Fight for Sex Workers' Rights* (2020) by Molly Smith and Juno Mac) or where sex workers are co-authors or chapter contributors (for example, in *Sex Work Matters: Exploring Money, Power, and Intimacy in the Sex Industry* (2010) by Melissa Ditmore and colleagues). In early reviews of the proposal for this book, I was asked whether I would consider co-authorship with someone working in the sex industry. This raises a critical question about authorship, particularly academic authorship, and power. Who would be next to me co-writing the book, challenging my selection choices, interpretation and presentation? However, aside from the data protection challenges of seeking to bring in a participant as a co-author, the truth was that I did not know my participants: I had never met them in person and for many I had only an email, sometimes a first name, if they shared it. Having gone through over 500 survey responses from those involved in the sex industry in the first part of the Home Office research (see Chapter 2), I also knew that opinions and experiences were diverse, often conflicting. What I really needed was for *all* my participants to share in the writing and reviewing of the book. So that is what I decided to try and do.

2

Methods and Ethics

This chapter explains how the data was collected and analysed and so is important in assessing what we can learn about the sex industry from the participant accounts in this book, the limitations, and what areas and questions require further consideration. It comprises seven sub-sections: Data sampling and collection; Using email interviews; Ethics; Positionality; Narrative framework analysis; Participant involvement; and Chapter and book structure.

Data sampling and collection

The wider Home Office research, from which the accounts presented in this book emerge, involved a number of strands. It started by searching available literature in the UK and internationally which described the nature and prevalence of prostitution and sex work rather than, for example, discussions of policy. There are two limitations to academic literature in this area: first, the breadth of our collective knowledge depends on which groups involved in selling or buying sex academic researchers choose to focus on, and indeed who they can practically and ethically access. For example, the literature was until relatively recently dominated by studies of street sex workers, even though this group represent a small proportion of the overall population engaged in selling sex. A second issue is that funding capture and publication timescales are long. Important UK studies into new areas have emerged: these include the Beyond the Gaze project (2015–2018) led by Professor Teela Sanders, exploring online sex work; Dr Katy Pilcher's work on strip clubs and erotic performance (2012a, 2012b, 2017); Professor Tracey Sagar's study into student sex work (Sagar et al, 2015; Sagar et al, 2016); and Dr Max Morris' (2018) work on incidental sex work among young men. Notwithstanding these and other emerging studies, in spring 2018 when we were doing our initial searches, it felt that the available research did not in sufficient volume reflect the fast-changing reality of the sex industry. To understand the current picture, we needed to hear from those directly involved.

For this reason, we decided to launch an anonymous online survey asking a small number of open questions, calling on people to share their knowledge, their experience and suggest readings and key figures to speak to. The survey was left open for six months and yielded 1,180 responses, including 529 who identified as currently or recently involved in prostitution and sex work. Of the 529 survey respondents who had direct experience of the sex industry, I emailed 135 to invite them to complete further in-depth questions by email. Forty-two were completed and returned. Conscious that this online approach would likely exclude certain groups, we also sent out hard-copy questionnaires to 76 NGOs working with or representing those involved in selling sex to administer to their service-users or members to complete by hand. Nineteen were completed and returned. We also held email, face-to-face and group consultations and discussions in four cities across England and Wales with over 90 organizations including sex worker collectives, support services, police forces, adult services websites, health and local authorities, as well as leading academics, at different stages of the research. Prior to publishing the report, we asked the Home Office for permission to share a copy of the report pre-publication with contributors, including around 10–12 sex worker participants. This led to some very useful final edits where statutory, third sector, academic or research participants had particular observations or wanted issues further clarified. I want to reflect briefly here on using email to interview.

Using email interviews

In terms of a data collection method, Burns (2010) describes his experience of the email interview as an 'irregularity', a stand-in when participants could not attend a face-to-face interview. This phrase captures very well how the email interview perhaps emerged by accident in early studies, rather than being selected purposefully as a method. Hershberger and Kavanaugh (2017) interviewed two groups about reproductive health decision-making and gave participants a choice of phone or email interview. Thirty-one per cent opted for email. When comparing the data yielded from the two modes of interview, Hershberger and Kavanaugh found that 'in-depth, asynchronous email interviews were appropriate and garnered rich, insightful data' (2017, p 50). Using email interviews in a qualitative research study with women who had experienced perinatal loss, Ratislavová and Ratislav (2014) found that women appreciated the relative anonymity afforded by using email. It is for similar reasons that researchers on sensitive topics have found phone interviews useful: there is something potentially freeing and enabling for some participants, not to have to look eye-to-eye with a researcher. For others of course, that in-person connection is important. In terms of data quality, Ratislavová and Ratislav found that '[t]he nature of the response, however, varies—it is often denser, more structured and more explicit compared to face-to-face interviews. Participants have more time to think and consider their answers and can review their responses and reflect on them, which helps them engage in more careful communication' (2014, p 454).

For me, it was this ability for participants to craft their responses that was significant: it was clear from the many rich responses that participants had spent time making sense of their own experiences on paper. Potentially too, this empowered participants because they had version control of the final submitted narrative. In a live interview, participants may be exploring their thoughts and feelings for the first time and, while that is also intensely valuable to researchers, it limits the opportunities to have some time to reflect and change the record – "I am not sure I quite meant that". Open methods, where interview transcripts are shared with participants to enable edits, do allow for this. However, sharing transcripts does not often happen, partly due to the time constraints of funded research and partly perhaps because researchers worry that those participants will be more likely to seek to withdraw parts or all of their interview (which is their right, at any time, under General Data Protection Regulations [GDPR]).

Since in this research the emailed interview questions were sent and completed once and did not involve a back-and-forth clarification of their responses, it could be argued that they should more accurately be described as a qualitative survey method. This is a valid observation. However, I think the act of inviting and then corresponding one-on-one by email with a participant does create a different dynamic to an anonymous survey. I also believe it would not have been feasible to engage in lengthy clarifications on email, for this project at least, out of respect for participants' unpaid time and patience. The value of the email interview may in part depend on literacy and both the use of online and writing-focused methods place barriers for some potential participants, which in turn affects the representativeness of the sample. At the same time, it was not necessarily the most literate or lengthy responses that were the most powerful. In summary, the value and potential flexibilities of email interviews for future research – particularly for individuals and groups who prefer to maintain anonymity – make it an effective method of choice.

Ethics

The original Home Office research was granted ethical approval by a University of Bristol research ethics committee. Under GDPR, researchers are able to re-use anonymized research data, where it is in the public interest, and where the identities of participants and the data security continue to be protected. However, I felt more comfortable seeking explicit consent from the participants to re-use the email interview data, partly because I wanted to use more extensive (albeit still anonymous) extracts from the email interviews, and partly because they had written it for one purpose, and I was now looking to re-use the data for another format. In addition, I wanted to conduct follow-up interviews by email to invite the participants to reflect on being involved in the Home Office study and to ask about their experiences during COVID-19. I also wanted to ask if they would, in principle, like to be involved in reviewing sections of the book before publication.

I therefore sought renewed ethical approval from the University and contacted 31 of the original 42 email participants: selected to ensure a balance across different settings and different genders. It is important to note here that this data therefore comes from the email group and not from the 19 hard-copy questionnaires distributed through NGOs. Eighteen of the 31 participants invited responded and agreed to have their data re-used and 17 within this group agreed to engaging in follow-up work for the book; one had left the industry and emigrated but was happy for their original data to be used. Eleven did not reply at all; one requested further information but then did not email again; and one email address was no longer working. The longer excerpts in this book therefore draw from these 18 respondents; selected short quotes are used from the remaining dataset, with care and where appropriate. Of the 17 who agreed in principle to answer follow-up questions, 16 did so. In addition, 16 participants were invited to review chapters because longer excerpts from their first or second interviews had been used; 14 provided chapter feedback. Figure 2.1 summarizes this process.

The research design and the approach to analysis chosen here are intimately tied to ethics and to my own epistemic interests. As explained in the previous section and in Chapter 1, I decided to seek a follow-up interview with participants to: (a) ask about their experience of being involved in, and represented through, government-funded research; and (b) to ask about their experience during COVID-19. This is because I was interested in whether they felt that participating had been 'worth it' (Did the report speak to their experience? Did it do so fairly and accurately? Did they feel it could lead to policy change? Would they participate in research again?) and I also wanted to know the 'after-story' (What had happened since? How did they reflect back on what they said in the first interview? Had anything changed?). It is that longitudinal, retrospective and reflexive perspective that is often lacking in current qualitative research: in part a function of the funding environment which drives academics to move on to the next project.

Positionality

The book was initially envisaged as an anthology pulling together the first interviews, perhaps interspersed with commissioned artwork. I have always been interested in writing – poetry, fiction, autobiography – as a form of

Figure 2.1: Participant sample and participation

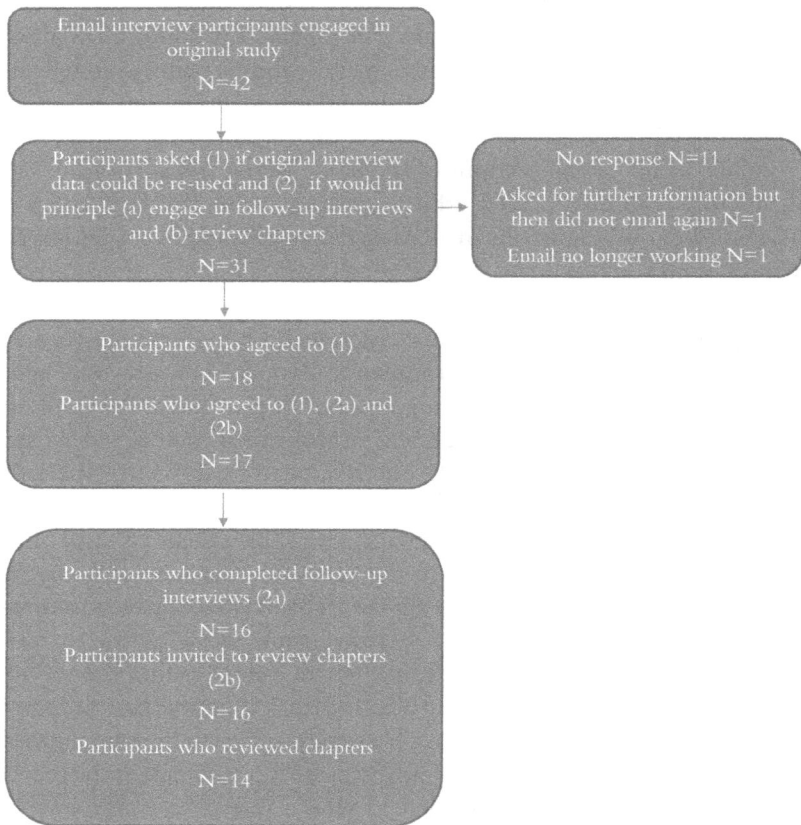

documenting lives and as an emancipatory act, following Freire (1970 [1996]). In my work as a researcher, I am mindful of the potential cathartic effects of narrative disclosure and of the responsibility of being given someone's story.

> Thank you for allowing me to complete this form. I appreciate you doing this research so thoroughly. In my experience, you only realise how prevalent sex work is once you become a sex worker. Because I'm out and often striving to get my voice heard, people reveal their histories of having done or doing sex work. They may never have told anyone before and often ask me to keep it a secret, but it seems like a relief that they can tell someone. (Female sex worker, working across multiple indoor settings)

> I have trusted you, to maybe help the vulnerable sex workers. To get more insight of prostitution. I do not want any trouble, so I trusted you. Thank you. (Female sex worker, working on street)

However, as acknowledged in Chapter 1, given technological developments and caution about 'expert power' there is no longer the same need for intermediaries, such as academics or practitioners, to lead such work. People can speak for themselves. But talking to my publisher, it quickly became clear that I would have to do more than catalogue: I needed to provide some comment and context.

Research is not a neutral endeavour: in writing about others, we tend to leave traces of ourselves. Researchers' worldviews or paradigms, it is argued, 'determine the kind of questions researchers ask, how these questions are to be understood, what data to collect, and how to interpret research results to derive answers to these questions' (Bergman, 2010, p 172). Therefore, in the drafting stage, I asked the research participants to read their chapter, including my commentary, and provide feedback and edits: to be a critical voice. This is explained further under the sub-heading 'Participant involvement'.

Narrative framework analysis

To present and explore the participant stories, I used what I will call 'narrative framework analysis'. This approach is influenced by interpretivist and constructionist paradigms (Hammersley, 1992). Interpretivist research seek to make sense of 'the complex world of lived experience from the point of view of those who live it' (Schwandt, 1998, p 221). This approach accepts that individual perceptions both differ and matter: 'The knowledge arising from interpretivist research is integrally linked to the participants and the context of the research, meaning that the products of interpretivist research are not universally applicable theories or laws but, rather, rich and contextually situated understandings' (McChesney and Aldridge, 2019, p 227). In this book, elements of two methods of analysis were combined – 'narrative' and 'framework'. Before I outline each in turn, I should acknowledge clearly that when the first interview data was collected, it was not conducted as a narrative or life-history interview. It was a set of questions devised to better understand current experiences of the sex industry (see Appendix 4 in Hester et al, 2019). The narrative approach has therefore been retrofitted to these interviews.

Heath (1986, p 84) defines the narrative as 'verbalized memories of past or ongoing experiences'. Narratives, including self-narratives (Gergen, 1994), are actively and purposefully constructed by the narrator:

> In developing a self-narrative, we establish coherent connections among life events (Cohler, 1982; Kohli, 1981). Rather than see our life as 'one damned thing after another', we formulate a story in which life events are systematically related, rendered intelligible by their place in a sequence or 'unfolding process' (de Waele and Harré, 1976). Our

present identity is thus not a sudden and mysterious event but a sensible result of a life story. (Gergen, 1994, in Wetherell et al, 2005, p 248)

I remember first reading this passage by Gergen and being struck by its simple insight. Our life stories are not a self-evident sequence of events; rather they are the retrospective selection of events which we choose to remember and articulate because we believe they are important and because we think they say something about who we are now. Self-narratives are therefore a meaning-making process (Çalişkan, 2018, p 10): they visibilize how we make coherent and account for our experiences, actions or inactions. This means also that 'narratives speak truth even when they include factual errors' (Çalişkan, 2018, p 11) because they are about opening a window on the narrator's constructions of the social world and their lives within it.

Qualitative analysis commonly involves coding and grouping excerpts from, for example, an interview transcript, and often cross-comparing these excerpts with those from other interviews. In narrative analysis, however, there is a concern to keep accounts intact because their overall shape and features are important to the analysis (Riessman, 1993). In this way, narrative analysis responds to the concern that in breaking up qualitative data, we risk decontextualizing and potentially misinterpreting. This is again good reason why there is value in going back to research participants to check that they are not misquoted. However, with a large dataset, it can be helpful to use both 'whole text' and 'excerpt' analysis, and this is the approach I take in this book. For each chapter, therefore, extended passages from the original email interviews are presented and commented on, but the commentaries also include brief discussion of quotes from other email interviews, using a framework approach.

Framework analysis was developed by Ritchie and Spencer (1994) and is used commonly in social and health research. It involves familiarization with the data and identifying meaningful categories to manage the data (the 'framework'). The data itself is pieced out into categories ('indexed'), can be summarized ('charted') and finally mapped and interpreted. It has some commonality then with qualitative content analysis (Mayring, 2000) and is in some ways distinctly anti-narrative! However, by holding on to the participants' original words and importing extended passages into the framework, this is a practical means of analysing a large dataset. The five framework categories identified for this study were identified from the original email interview questions (see Appendix 4 of Hester et al, 2019).

The commentary sections in each chapter are not a 'critique' of the narrative accounts: rather I am summarizing and reflecting on how participants make sense of their own experience and, where appropriate, making links to existing studies.

Participant involvement

There is a well-established literature on participant and community involvement in research (for example, Smith, 1994; Baum et al, 2006; Mulvihill et al, 2011). 'Involvement' can range from being involved in identifying research questions and topics, through to designing method, to checking transcripts and draft findings (termed 'member checking'), to being involved in designing outputs, dissemination, evaluation and implementation of findings. Participants may be co-investigators and co-authors, may sit on a research advisory group or act more informally as critical friends. I want to discuss two issues briefly here: the experience of being involved in research and asking participants to review draft findings.

First, Dennis (2014, p 397) notes that while academic ethics committees require us to take participant wellbeing into account, in the sense that we 'do no harm', fewer studies have asked participants about their experience of participating in research and how it matched their expectations. McCoyd and Shdaimah identify three reasons articulated by participants for being involved:

> (1) the validation of being understood and of having one's story heard in full without judgment; (2) the chance to have one's story joined with others in such a way as to create a 'voice' on a topic of shared experiences, and (3) the knowledge that findings will be published and communicated to providers, policymakers, and the public. (2007, p 347)

Sometimes, when researchers are funded for 'impact work', data is gathered on how participants felt about their experience of engaging in the research. However, while it may be easier to evidence (1) and (2), the timescales for policy and practice impact are longer and gauging how participants, in retrospect, feel about (3) is more challenging. For example, 'Yes the findings were published and disseminated: but did anything then change?' For this reason, I ask the participants in the follow-up interview the questions shown in Table 2.1.

A second issue is what is often called 'member checking'. This is where participants are asked, for example, to check their interview transcripts and provide corrections or clarifications or to read draft findings before publication. Ostensibly, the goal of member checking is to enhance the credibility and validity of qualitative research (Lincoln and Guba, 1985) although researchers are not always explicit in their write-up how that supposition works in practice (Birt et al, 2016, p 1803). For example, Thomas (2017, p 39) suggests that where research is concerned particularly in ensuring *accurate representation* of participants' perspectives or experiences [then] 'selective use of member checks may be justified.' However, member checking can raise further practical and ethical issues too: participants may

Table 2.1: Follow-up email interview questions

1	Reading back through your original email interview, how do you reflect on what you wrote?
2	Is there anything you would now add? Has anything changed? You might want to speak here too about the impact of COVID-19 on you and your work, and/or what it has demonstrated in terms of policy and protecting sex workers, and so on.
3	What was your experience of participating in the Home Office 2019 study? Did you feel your opinions and experiences were reflected in the final report? [You can be as critical as you like here.] What are your reflections on how sex workers and the sex industry are engaged in, and represented through, academic and government research?

not engage in checking, or only in very small numbers, and checking requests are an additional intrusion and demand on the unpaid time of participants (Thomas, 2017). Further, what do you do when a participant strongly disagrees with your findings: do you re-write them? And does that make them more credible? And what if another participant disagrees with the re-write? For a number of reasons, therefore, academics have expressed scepticism about such approaches (see Morse, 2015).

In this book, I invited the participants whose individual (and anonymized) stories I drew on at length, to comment on the draft chapters. My aim in this was partly to give participants the opportunity to correct or comment on any misrepresentation, but also to open up the research process to the readers of this book. I wanted to visibilize that 'this is a contested area and here are the points of contestation, but also of consensus too'. This approach is therefore more consistent with Tracy's description of 'member reflections' (2010):

> [M]ember reflections are less a test of research findings as they are an opportunity for collaboration and reflexive elaboration. Member reflections ... help the researcher learn whether members find the research comprehendible and meaningful. Through the reflection process, participants can react, agree, or find problems with the research. ... Participants may argue against findings at one point, and endorse them down the line—for any number of personal or political reasons. The researcher has very little control over participants' reactions, or the ways research is eventually evaluated or used. However, they do have control in providing the space and option for member reflections, and in doing so, provide opportunities for additional data and elaboration that will enhance the credibility of the emerging analysis. (Tracy, 2010, p 844)

In Chapter 8, I discuss the participant reviews of their chapters and reflect on the value of that process as an author.

Chapter and book structure

The remainder of the book is split into six chapters, each focusing on a different part of the sex industry: Chapter 3 on female independent sex work; Chapter 4 on male independent sex work; Chapter 5 on working in managed brothels and parlours; Chaper 6 on erotic dancing and stripping; and Chapter 7 on paying for sexual services and intimacy. Narratives are presented as they were written by the participant; ellipses in square brackets ([...]) recognize where elements of the text were edited out for reasons of chapter word count or repeated points already made. The final chapter, Chapter 8, draws together reflections on the method and the contribution of this book.

Each chapter follows a particular structure: it opens with an extended extract from the original participant interviews followed by a commentary built around the framework categories. The findings from the follow-up interviews are then presented and discussed, before a chapter summary.

3

Female Independent Sex Workers

While it is near impossible to discern the exact national population of sex workers at any given time (Vandepitte et al, 2006; Hester et al, 2019, pp 35–40 and 59–66), within that elusive overall number, proportionately women constitute the majority of those selling sex. This applies in the UK and globally and includes here trans women and individuals designated female at birth who do not recognize a binary gender identity, but who may present as female for the purpose of selling sex (for more on the experiences of trans women and non-binary people selling sex, see: Brown et al, 2010; D'Ippoliti and Botti, 2017; Samudzi, 2017; Nuttbrock and Bockting, 2018; Van Schuylenbergh et al, 2018; Orchard et al, 2020).

Women may sell sex (often termed 'full-service' sex work) or provide sexual or erotic services (such as erotic massage) directly in-person, or online (such as through webcamming). An 'escort' is someone who is engaged in full-service sex work: they may work independently or be employed through an agency. BDSM refers to bondage, domination, sadism (or submission) and masochism and can be a specific service offered by 'professional dominatrices' or 'submissives', for example. Some escorts may also provide BDSM services as part of their overall offer. Erotic masseurs provide massage, commonly including masturbation of the client. This service may be organized by individuals themselves or through intermediaries. Examples of third parties include managed brothels, parlours, agencies or working for/being coerced by a pimp or partner/pimp.

This chapter focuses on independent female sex workers. This group may work from home, rent their own permanent premises, or use hotels/apartments and manage the money themselves. Outdoor (or 'street') workers may also be independent workers, and some will organize their work through the internet or using a mobile phone. Increasingly, independent workers are using adult services websites to run a profile to attract clients, and some may also have their own website or social media account (Cunningham et al, 2018). The majority of women's clients are men (National Surveys of Sexual Attitudes and Lifestyles, 1990 to date: see, for example, Ward et al,

2005) and this reflects the prevailing set of gender relations dominant in most societies. Some women also provide services to couples and a smaller number to other women (Kingston et al, 2020). The interviews demonstrate that the gender of clients is not necessarily linked to the sex worker's personal sexual orientation.

Part of the reason that discerning precise numbers of individuals involved in sex work is difficult is that the ascription of the term 'sex worker' is disputed (see Hester et al, 2019, pp 9–11). For example, someone may occasionally exchange money for sex to make ends meet or they may work in the sex industry but not provide 'full-service' or they may be experiencing chaotic homelessness, trauma and substance misuse and exchanging sex for drugs: individuals in these contexts may not identify their practices with the term 'sex work'. In addition, individuals may move into sex working for a short period to see them through a difficult financial period or may engage intermittently over time, yet also have other income, through other paid work or benefits, for example. Again, this means that the population of those engaged in 'sex work', however defined, is constantly shifting.

It is important not to conflate 'working independently' with 'choice' or, indeed the opposite, to assume that sex work 'cannot be independently chosen' (see Mulvihill, 2019, for further discussion on this). As the stories and reflections in this book demonstrate, choice, agency, constraint and coercion (either interpersonally by other individuals or structurally through personal and economic contexts) can co-occur in seeming contradiction, and indeed may shift over time for the same individual. Such contradictions are not exclusive to sex workers.

Participant narratives (original email interview)

In this section are presented longer narratives from Rosalind (an erotic masseur); Cordelia (an independent escort); Beatrice (a professional dominatrix); Helena (an independent sex worker and adult content provider); and Blake (an independent escort and former sugar baby). The excerpts are followed by discussion, drawing in also brief quotes from experiences from other participants who gave first interviews in the original research.

Rosalind's story (female erotic masseur)

I started in late 2013 as an escort (independent) and 2017 I switched to erotic massage. As an escort I offered full service. I chose this work because I wanted to be my own boss and I always found the sex industry alluring. It was an adventure and self-exploration as well as a financial endeavour.

I had a friend, who used to work as a gay escort — he gave me a lot of useful advice before I started; I also looked for advice online. It took me around a month to prepare and start escorting. Initially I used [online classified site], then [an adult service website]. I have always worked independently.

I work full-time, however, I've always struggled with being consistent with working hours due to emotional issues, which have always been a problem in my life. Thanks to sex work and being my own boss, I can arrange the work schedule according to how I feel: it's a blessing. I only accept cash and handle it myself. I take cash at the beginning of the booking.

I used to work and study at the same time, but eventually I dropped out from the course.

It's been almost 2 years that I've worked as an erotic masseuse and I definitely prefer what I do now. I can set up boundaries that I couldn't when offering a full service. [...] I would say that the main demographics are men between 35–55 years old, but they really are a mix — all races and nationalities (mainly Caucasian and English/European though), various occupations (from office workers, people who are well off to tradesmen).

There is a difference between the clients I had as an escort and now that I do erotic massage only. They don't see it as cheating as much. It's more respectful of my own boundaries. I get to choose if I want to be naked or not, if I want to be touched and how much; in general, the clients are rather passive and respectful.

[Massage is] less emotionally and physically draining. I talk much less with my clients, which also is less draining at the end of the day.

I charge much less than I used to as an escort, but I find it more sustainable, and I am able to do more bookings (and I have to work more as my bills are the same as they were as an escort). I don't have to pretend that I'm enjoying myself, or force myself to enjoy myself, so to speak. Massage is focused on the clients — it's a one-way thing — and I prefer it much more. I also feel like I can be more caring and giving towards them; I don't have to protect myself as much.

I find this job very enjoyable. There is so much to learn with bodywork — different types of massages. So many things to do to innovate and improve! [...] Also, there is less shame and stigma, which helps so much. It still is a sex service, sex work, but milder and more innocent, somehow.

I feel like it's a bit of a creative outlet. I learn a lot about business, people, marketing, IT (I did my own website). It's satisfying in so many ways. It makes me feel happy, needed. It gives me a purpose in life and pride, too. The whole sex business has a level of fun and absurdity that I find very compelling.

Without it, at the moment, I don't know what I would do.

I think [what I do] is adding value to my clients' lives. There is a physical and sexual aspect to this, but also emotional and human. They leave me happy (well, that's my impression and that's what they often say) and smiling, and it's very rewarding.

Sex is a basic human need, and not everyone is lucky enough to have this need met.

[What are the challenges and risks?] Physical safety. As sex workers we are considered easy prey; there is always fear of being attacked, robbed, stalked.

Shame and the need to be silent about this job, living a double life to some extent, because of the stigma attached to this.

It's extremely difficult to have a personal life, a romantic relationship or just regular relationships with people, meeting new people, who you just don't know if they are judgemental or if you can trust them.

The harm would probably be that I feel like damaged goods now – if I was looking for a meaningful romantic relationship, it really weighs down on my self-esteem.

I'm less trustful of men now. But more realistic about them, probably.

I'm not planning too much ahead as I'm doing therapy at the moment, to deal with my upbringing, which is essentially at the core of the emotional issues that thwart my life.

Sex work is a blessing: it gives me space and an opportunity to deal with these issues at my own pace, and to be able to afford the help that I need.

Cordelia's story (female independent escort)

I view myself as an escort/sex worker, providing intimate/sexual services for men in exchange for money.

In mid-2014, I was made redundant from a well-paid job I'd had for 17 years. I wanted to set myself up as a freelancer in the same industry but knew that would a) take time and b) not pay very well. So, as I was also single at the time, I decided to take a few months off 'civvy' work completely and try my hand at escorting. I put up a profile on [an adult service website] and a few other places, and within a few weeks also created my own website, bought a second, [pay-as-you-go] mobile and started seeing clients within a day or two of having the profiles and phone set up.

I have my own website, Twitter, and profiles on [an adult service website]. [...] I will accept emails, texts, and messages on Twitter, websites and fora in terms of booking enquiries, but I always insist on a phone call before any booking is confirmed. I take cash as soon as the client arrives. No one else ever has been or ever will be involved in how I work as an escort!

I always work alone [and] I don't know any other sex workers in real life, i.e., only online.

Most of the time I enjoy the sex. The money is an important part of my total income. As I work from home in my civvy job, and have just relocated to an area where I don't know anyone, escorting also provides some company and social interaction to break up the day. I enjoy meeting new clients and getting to know those who become regulars. I'm also active on a couple of online fora dedicated to sex work, which are useful and/or entertaining.

I used to live and work in a very wealthy part of [England], but my clients were from all backgrounds, wealth levels etc. I don't see certain clients based on age (over 60) or country of origin (from the Indian sub-continent or sub-Saharan Africa); I do see British/Western-born men of all ethnicities. Some men are very attractive and/or successful, others less so. Levels of sexual experience and skill also vary hugely. I have taken the virginity of a couple of men and also seen men with disabilities/health problems, and it is very satisfying to be able to help them. It's always nice to send more general clients away with a smile on their face!

Physical safety is always a concern, though so far, I have had no problems. I work from home, which does leave me a little exposed, though only one client has ever turned up unannounced, and I am careful to be discreet. I'm a tenant, not a home-owner, so need to be cautious. Timewasters are a huge pain, and obviously some bookings can be difficult, maybe even unpleasant.

I hope to continue escorting part-time alongside my civvy job for as long as health and other factors allow.

I am strongly pro-decriminalisation and very anti the Nordic model. Sex workers should be allowed to work together for improved safety, and no changes made to current online platforms that help with our screening and security. It is also extremely vexing when prostitution is conflated with trafficking.

Trafficking/slavery is horrific, and the strongest measures should be taken to stamp it out, but many British women work happily as independent sex workers, and we should be allowed to do so.

Beatrice's story (female professional dominatrix)

I started fetish modelling aged 17 after a photographer friend helped me build a portfolio, and then I began advertising online. At 21 I progressed to sugaring and then at 22, went on to offer domination services.

This work started as being part-time, as I was a full-time student and then a freelance creative. At 24, it became my sole income and has remained as such up until the present day [now mid–30s]. Intermittent/ part-time working was always necessary to boost my income, and then when it has become my sole income it has helped while I have had to save up money to escape an abusive ex/pimp, and at another point had to be a full-time carer. And at other points, due to mental ill health, it's been important for me to be able to work in ways that support my recovery or at least help me to manage my symptoms. I still do freelance creative work occasionally when I am well enough, but it is not a predictable or reliable source of income.

I have always organised the work myself. […] I now only deal with incoming emails from clients through my website, and then have a phone consultation in order to work out suitability and safety in seeing them.

I take a deposit in advance if it's a new client, and the remainder is settled in cash. I don't split this with anyone, but I do have a work premises, so this obviously takes up a fair amount of my running costs. For a few years in my twenties my 'partner'/pimp took half my earnings. Although they contributed no time to doing any of the organizing, it did mean that someone was at the premises while I worked. They did also check the email account and phone to monitor my communications though, and choose who I was or wasn't allowed to see – more for their own selfish reasons than for my safety, I suspect.

With a friend there I'd feel safer to see a new client or a client that had a slight red flag, and there's certainly clients I've only been willing to accept as a duo. With a friend, we can catch up afterwards and have a laugh about the session, and wind down. On my own, although I'm fine with it, I do get quite isolated since I'm working from home and sometimes am too depressed to leave the house when I've finished work.

[My clients are] mostly in their 40s, 50s, and 60s, White British, well-spoken, well-educated, middle class professional men. I think they come to me for a release and an escape from their normal life, and to explore an aspect of their sexuality that they don't think could be satisfied elsewhere.

[In terms of the benefits], it has been a way of surviving while being disabled, since I can work for only a few hours a week or even a few hours a month if that's all I can manage, and [still be able] to pay the rent. A way of learning a lot about sexuality, the human body, and trust since I really do see people at their most vulnerable and sensitive sometimes. It's helped me work through some of my male-related trauma at times. For my non sex working friends, I've become an expert in so many subjects and help people to open up and talk without shame about the body, desires and sexuality. For clients, some have told me I have provided an intense form of therapy. I've been told more than once that I've kept someone from suicide. I've also helped clients work through and get rid of their shame around sex, queerness and abuse.

[In terms of risks] even though I am working from a commercial property, I still have to hide what I do from the council and my landlord. I also know the immense amount of emotional labour that my work requires, and I have to be extremely careful to not let it impact me too much. I also need to be careful about sexual health [and] use a sex work friendly clinic for sexual health testing. I also consider myself totally unemployable now, such is the stigma of sex work. I don't have a plan B for what to do next, and I've already got burnout more than once. I also have to be careful with clients that demand risky BDSM services.

I am saving up money so that when my future plan is clear, I can put it into action. It's hard for me to imagine my creative pursuits ever being viable full-time, and I'm not confident enough to take that risk to launch into them fully with my savings to support me – since this would be a limited amount of money.

Please support the decriminalisation of sex work! Lack of information and having to tiptoe around the broken legal system is what makes a lot of sex workers feel so vulnerable. I'm sure I wouldn't have got myself into such a horrible situation with a pimp when I was younger if the conditions were better for me to simply do my work. At times my work has been survival sex work, and this is a dire situation that no one should have to be in – although it also makes me very grateful for being able to do sex work and avoid total destitution.

Helena's story (female independent escort and adult content provider)

Started beginning of 2015. Was employed full-time in a relatively senior management role in a large international [company]. One month I was having a cash crisis and was looking for ways to make extra money quickly. Came across a blog post about webcam work and decided to try it.

Found I really enjoyed being on cam, and as a plus size mature woman I found the confidence boost amazing. […] Lots of cam guys would ask 'Do you meet?' and I always said 'No', but one day I thought, 'Maybe I should try it – if I don't like it, then I never have to do it again, and nobody has to know'. So, I switched my profile to offering escort services and had my first booking within about 4 hours!

I went full-time escorting in 2016 and initially I would be available every day, but I now work Thursday to Tuesday every week and take

Wednesdays off. When I am working, I am generally available 6am to 8pm and I accept bookings of a length between 15 minutes and 2 hours. All appointments are arranged by telephone call or text to my mobile.

[Have you experienced other sectors of the sex industry?] I have done phone chat with a premium rate service based in the UK but found the work too patchy. I've also webcammed on an American site but dislike the culture of these sites that basically forces providers to beg for tips. I felt like a performing seal.

I work alone. I would share an apartment if I knew someone really well and it wasn't a 'known' apartment for sex workers, as these are very often targeted for robbery and/or assault. Working in hotels makes me feel safer.

This work can be isolating so I would prefer working with others in a set-up such as a workers' cooperative with a receptionist, cleaning staff, security staff, CCTV, etc. I think many women would feel much happier working like this and it would also help outdoor workers get off the streets. But as the law stands, that is illegal as it would be controlling prostitution. So, the current laws make sex workers less safe already.

Most of the friends that I've met through networking with other [sex workers] (primarily via online forums) tend to be quite similar to myself – mid 30s and older, got kids at home, not interested in partying or taking drugs, quite organised in terms of savings plans, paying tax, etc.

We swap information about dangerous or time-wasting clients and we find that we have very similar experiences. We all are quite security conscious, so we don't tend to encounter too many dangerous types (if you consider the numbers against our total footfall).

[In terms of benefits of this work] I have the freedom of self-employment – I can see who I want, where I want, when I want, and for what services I want. If I don't like a client, I never have to see him again. My earnings are directly related to how hard I work – I'm not putting money in someone else's pocket, busting my arse to get results and then getting paid the same salary as someone who's doing the bare minimum.

Sex work has been a massive help with being able to set boundaries – because if you can't set and keep boundaries, you will start hating the job and the clients very soon. I have much more confidence now to say, 'I'm not comfortable with this' and, if necessary, 'I've told you to stop already. If you do it again, I will end the booking and you will be leaving without a refund'. In my civvy life, I often felt unable to assert myself and would just go along with whatever a sexual partner wanted, feeling that I couldn't speak up and say, 'I'm not into this, let's do something else'.

In terms of my clients, I know that in many cases I am the only intimate physical touch they experience, being either single or widowed. I see quite a few clients who have physical challenges such as morbid obesity, erectile dysfunction, partial paralysis/mobility issues, or mental health issues such as low self-esteem, anxiety, autism spectrum disorder, depression and chronic stress.

The one thing a client has said that's stuck with me was a guy who was undergoing chemo (although I didn't know this until after the sex part of the booking was finished). He said, 'Thank you so much – you've made me feel like a human being again instead of just a collection of symptoms'.

[And the risks?] Every time we put ourselves naked and alone in a room with a stranger, we're taking a risk. Most of us have developed systems to minimise those risks as much as possible, but still, it's there. We could be robbed, raped, physically assaulted or even killed. It's wrong that the law doesn't allow us the basic protections that working together would provide.

In addition to risks from clients, we also face stigma and shame from those outside the industry. Many sex workers have been outed to friends, family and partners and some have been outcast from their communities and/or families, threatened with, 'I'll have the kids taken off you', etc. I know two sex workers who have been fired from their civvy jobs after vindictive arses decided to report them to their companies.

Self-employment also comes with its own set of risks. No holiday pay, no sick pay. If we don't work, we can't pay the bills. If we get injured, we could face weeks without pay. Most of us take some steps to ameliorate these risks – private health insurance, a 'rainy day' fund, etc – but we are generally unable to take out income protection insurance in the same way that, say, a self-employed gardener could.

Relationships with friends and family can often suffer. I have a small but close circle of family and friends who are aware of what I do and are supportive. I have withdrawn from all those who I think would disapprove of me doing this work.

I have become much warier and more cynical and find myself constantly risk-assessing every situation, which can be exhausting.

My current strategy is to continue sex work as long as physically possible – I'm hoping I've got at least another 15–20 years. Exit strategy will be property management but if this doesn't look viable as I get closer, I'll probably be looking to train as a therapist, considering a significant proportion of our work is emotional labour.

Blake's story (non-binary independent escort and former sugar baby)

I was forced to drop out of university for financial reasons (if whoever is doing this research is able to influence policy, please fix student finance), and needed to find a source of income to stay in the city where I studied. I chose sex work, essentially, because I felt it was better than cleaning or waitressing. I also chose it because I have a number of health issues, which in combination mean that working full-time hours can be fairly detrimental to my physical health. [...]

I enjoy the amount of freedom it gives me. I like having the ability to choose my own working hours and to use my time off to pursue hobbies. [...] It's also fun having a job that lets me meet people, as I occasionally have pretty interesting conversations with them. Sex work also allows me to make money as and when I need it, rather than being dependent on a monthly wage, which is good, because I can't budget for shit. [...]

I was briefly a sugar baby while I was at uni. I would say that this can possibly be more financially productive than other types of sex work (if you're lucky), but I found it financially unreliable and emotionally draining. There is a lot more emotional labour that goes into sugaring than escorting, as you are expected to build (or at least act) a relationship with your clients. In addition, as there is a smaller client base (maybe even only one), it is less financially stable, and I disliked feeling dependent on someone else paying me – a big part of the appeal of sex work for me is that I am the only person in charge of what I do, and you don't have that in the same way as a sugar baby. [...]

On a personal level, I am nonbinary and DFAB [designated female at birth] and advertise as a cis woman, because people expect sex workers to be cis women and it gets me more business than being honest. But portraying myself as something I don't identify with, and the very gendered way in which sex work is talked about, can be dysphoria-inducing for me. [...]

I mostly work alone, though I do duo bookings with a friend of mine at times. I am happy with either, though working predominantly alone does occasionally make me feel lonely. Most of my friends have full-time jobs or are students so it means I often don't get much social interaction, which I would have otherwise had through work colleagues.

[In the future] I'd like to publish more books and finish my degree at some point. I will probably keep escorting on the side until I get too old though, because it's fun and a good source of income.

Discussion of first interviews

In this section, I discuss both the narratives presented in the previous section and draw on the wider first interview data. This analysis is set out in five parts, as explained in Chapter 2, namely: routes in; benefits; harms; hoped-for changes in the industry; and future plans.

The narratives in the previous section and interviews with the wider participant group reveal a number of different routes into sex work. These include: experiencing a temporary financial crisis through redundancy or other life change; experiencing cumulative and acute economic fragility through inability to access or claim support while being a solo parent, carer, disabled, a student, recent migrant, or undergoing gender transition; getting involved in other areas of the sex industry, through leisure or work experiences or peer introduction, and later moving into independent sex work (for example attending sex parties and 'turning a hobby into a living' or working initially as a maid); or being groomed or coerced into commercial sex. Some, like Beatrice, may meet and then manage to escape abusive partner-pimps and go on to work independently. For example:

> I once had a pimp to look after me: that did not go well. He is serving time and I managed to break free before I got passed on. [Now] I work on my own. (Female independent street worker)

As well as routes in, those early experiences may be significant in determining whether and how women continue sex working. Helena, for example, explained the exhilaration of being admired by clients in her first webcam experience and realizing how quickly she could earn money. Meeting respectful and non-threatening clients in those early meetings is also likely important:

> I was pleasantly surprised that the majority of clients are nice, polite and good-looking. (Female independent escort)

> I have been fortunate enough to not have faced any in-person violence from my clients. (Female independent escort)

One participant amusingly, but perceptively, challenged my choice of question wording:

> 'Recruited'? This isn't the marines. I chose this work due to a lack of other options. (Female independent escort)

That final phrase captures perfectly the contradiction highlighted in the opening to this chapter, that agency and constraint are not mutually exclusive: 'I *chose* this work due to *lack of other options*' (my emphasis).

Financial independence and flexibility were identified as key benefits of sex work. Some participants, for example, explained how they were caring for ill partners or family members or were managing their own issues with chronic pain, disability or a mental health condition which made holding down a regular full-time job – providing sufficient income to live – a challenge. Others said they enjoyed meeting new clients and, as Rosalind observed, the clients 'leaving happy'. Some participants stressed the therapeutic aspect of sex work, both for the worker and for the client. Beatrice described:

> For clients, some have told me I have provided an intense form of therapy, I've been told more than once that I've kept someone from suicide, I've also helped clients work through and get rid of their shame around sex, queerness and abuse.

Her comment that '[i]t's helped me work through some of my male related trauma at times' is particularly interesting given how commonly sex work is understood as engendering or compounding 'male related trauma'. In later email feedback on this chapter, Beatrice elaborated that she found the transactional nature of sex work 'made it easier to create a dialogue with these men in which I clearly state my boundaries, reminding them that the interaction can end at any time if they are not respected'. This was in contrast to some of her experiences of non-paid sex. Another research participant reflected that:

> For me, it's helped me build my confidence. [...] I feel that I am more of a sexual person than society thinks someone who was assigned female at birth should be, but now I don't really care so much about that, I'm a lot more unapologetically me now. (Female BDSM worker)

Little has been written about sex work as therapy, although there is some literature on BDSM (Lindemann, 2011), sexological bodywork or mindfulness (Thouin-Savard, 2019). It is critical though to reflect on how discourses of 'therapy' are employed, by whom, and why, as well as to recognize that such experiences will depend on individual context and may vary over time. For example:

> I am not going to wax lyrical about the benefits sex work might give to clients, emotional healing or any of that (I have done in the past). I have stopped caring about clients. There are just far too many bad ones. Sex work has made me tougher, and (selectively) kinder. (Female independent escort)

In terms of the challenges and harms, it is worth noting first that a few participants in the original study objected to being asked this question. The objection came from the belief that, by asking this question, there was an implicit assumption that sex work is harmful: that the question was political. I recognized this concern but, given the question came after one asking about the benefits and pleasures of their work, I felt confident that asking *both* allowed participants to express their individual experiences. In addition, it allowed sex workers to distinguish – as they saw fit – personal, intrinsic or contextual harms, the latter including policing practice, the prevailing legal regime and the acerbic public debate on the sex industry.

As well as concerns around physical safety, sexual health, robbery or stalking, participants identified threats to 'out' them, which are powerful precisely because of the social stigma attached to sex work.

> I have been the victim of a stalker, who reported me to the hotel I worked from and also shared private pictures of me. If that was a normal partner, I would have gone to the police for the threats he sent me, but I do not feel that I would be taken seriously as an escort. (Female independent escort and sugar baby)

Others identified damage to personal relationships and self-perception, as explained by Rosalind (female erotic masseur) in the previous section, who describes feeling 'less trustful' but 'more realistic' about men, but also worried about being 'damaged goods'. This stigma potentially had a long-term effect by 'closing off' future opportunities, in intimate relationships and in work. There is something strongly gendered too in how participants expressed that experience and more work on the differential impact of stigma on sex-working women and men is needed:

> The lack of further employment opportunities is a huge thing – it's totally contradictory because I'm at university which should give you a sign that I don't intend to do this forever, but it's basically been rendered my only choice at least until I find a charity/NGO with enough goodwill to hire a 'fallen woman'. (Female independent escort, in Hester et al, 2019, p 22)

Emotional and psychological harm were linked to feelings of agency. Helena illustrates (elsewhere in her interview) how economic precarity constrains agency:

> Sometimes, however, they ask for something you're not happy with, but don't feel able to turn down, perhaps due to needing the money. Doing that often can lead to mental health issues, if it goes on too long. (Female independent escort)

This is confirmed by another participant, who writes:

> I am also in the privileged position of not needing to take on just anyone who messages me, I can afford to say no if something doesn't feel right. But I'm fully aware that this luxury is often not afforded to other sex workers, particularly those who do sex work to survive. (Female independent BDSM worker)

Helena talks about having developed a heightened state of awareness ('find myself constantly risk-assessing every situation, which can be exhausting'). This sort of response is common to those who have experienced abuse and trauma, as victims or witnesses, including people working in occupations such as the police, military, paramedics or war correspondents (Hughes et al, 2012). For sex workers, working often in secrecy, negotiating stigma and negotiating risk of client abuse, of police or other professional intervention, can provoke hypervigilance, a feature of post-traumatic stress disorder.

A small number of participants in the Home Office study spoke about sugar dating. A sugar arrangement is where an individual enters into a 'mutually beneficial relationship with another, exchanging companionship and/or intimacy with economic security (including fixed monthly payments) or benefit in kind (such as a place to live)' (Hester et al, 2019, p 32). The research literature on sugar dating in the Western context is small but growing (for example, Nayar, 2017; Mulvihill and Large, 2019) and has some links to the literature on the 'girlfriend experience' (GFE) (for example, Milrod and Monto, 2012; Carbonero and Garrido, 2018) as well research in African (such as the 'aristo' phenomenon: Tade and Adekoya, 2012) and East Asian (notably 'compensated dating': Chu, 2018) contexts. Both current or former sugar babies or escorts providing a GFE talked of the emotional labour (Hochschild, 1993) and deep acting required in spending long periods of time with someone. For example:

> My personal experience is of stumbling into [sugaring], but I know, by proxy, that in this area there are a few girls approaching guys through dating sites to ask for a financial arrangement. On the specific sugaring sites, I have found a very, very small percentage of members truly want a sugar relationship. Most are looking to date, or, [to] get some kind of deal on an escort. I personally feel this is one of the most 'shady' ways of sex-work being advertised, as they encourage personal meetings. There is no way of checking the client/worker's credentials, no paper trail, no feedback to check. I feel the stigma attached to being a prostitute means that people look for less offensive synonyms, and in

doing so may be blurring the lines and making things more dangerous for themselves. (Female independent escort and sugar baby)

A leading sugar arrangement website claims it has a quarter of a million UK students registered, although it is not clear what proportion of those profiles are active or duplicate. Sugar dating is an area that deserves further research.

The majority of participants identified the decriminalization of sex workers, in particular the decriminalization of a small number of individuals working together, as a key route to reducing harm. Sharing premises in this way is currently criminalized under law in England and Wales as constituting a brothel. Most rejected the Nordic model, which criminalizes buyers (but not sellers), as likely only to further marginalize and endanger sex workers and as failing to address the social and economic reasons why many women sell sex in the first place. Female independent workers also expressed concern about the closure of adult service websites, which they identified as giving them control and enhancing safety.

Finally, participants were asked about their future plans. Those who worked in BDSM, in particular, were likely to say they hoped to develop their business further. Those working as independent escorts also said they were happy to continue, as long as health and stamina allowed, although they were concerned about further criminalization measures in the sector. Others mentioned creative pursuits (although these did not necessarily provide enough income), returning to study or pursuing massage or therapy training. All of these hopes however rested very much on financial and personal context:

I would ultimately love a cottage by the water somewhere beautiful, with maybe goats and some chickens. [...] I am very aware of my privilege within escorting. I have a platform, I'm openly out to everyone, I have legal status in the UK, good education, a whole toolbox of power privileges. (Female independent escort)

[My future plans are] bleak. I am a prostitute. What man would want me to become his wife? I am still good looking and clean. Making enough money to put a small amount away. I really don't know – can't answer that one. (Female independent street worker)

Participant reflections (second email interview)

This section presents second interviews with Cordelia, Beatrice, Helena and Blake conducted in spring 2021. Rosalind had since left the sex industry and moved abroad but gave permission for her first interview to be reproduced for the book.

Cordelia's reflection (female independent escort)

I think my answers reflect my quite pragmatic and matter-of-fact approach to sex work. I'm not ashamed of it, but neither do I feel 'empowered' by it. For me, it is (was?) just a useful source of income.

[How have things changed since the first interview?] Quite a lot has changed, yes! Over 2019, I continued to do very, very few bookings, mainly because my civvy job was very busy. I also had my last proper period in Christmas week of 2019, so declared myself post-menopausal as of New Year's Day 2021. I was very lucky in that I had very few symptoms, but did have a noticeable drop in libido, and it is only just beginning to return. Everything still 'works', and I still enjoy sex when I have it, but the urge to do so definitely dropped over 2019 and 2020.

Then COVID-19 overlapped with this to a large extent. As well as being early 50s with health vulnerabilities, my background is in microbiology and my job is in healthcare information, so I took the threat seriously, and locked myself down quite hard. I just did one booking with a regular in the early summer, and two with an old regular […] in the autumn, but have had no clients since the national lockdown in England in [early November 2020]. My civvy work has remained solidly busy, thankfully, over the pandemic period, so financially I have been OK. […]

While I understand a few self-employed people genuinely slip through the SEISS [self-employment income support scheme grants] net, I have no sympathy for those (indie escorts) who can't claim because they haven't paid their taxes. […] I think it's also highlighted a longstanding opinion I've had, which is that sex work is best done for a short period (i.e., two years max) full-time, or for a longer period part-time only. COVID-19 meant some women used to earning £1,000 a week or more suddenly had no or very little income, and some had not saved a penny. […]

Over the past 18 months or so I've become involved in the online women's rights movement, which obviously includes many radical feminists who are extremely anti sex work. I don't agree with them, but I can at least see some of their points, i.e., how many women enter prostitution entirely voluntarily – as I did – versus those who are driven to it out of financial desperation or are coerced by a man to do so? Ditto that women being available for sale enhances the risk of all women being seen as sexual commodities. I think I will always feel that women should have the opportunity to enter sex work if they wish to do so, but it would be great if no one felt they had to. I am, for example, a big supporter of a universal basic income.

A sort of side issue, but I really miss the Praed Street Project (PSP) that was run for sex workers at St Mary's Hospital, but closed when funding was ended and so sex workers were treated exactly the same as general public clients. Under the PSP I received the hepatitis B vaccine, some free treatments for minor issues, and was always asked how I was. [Where I live now], the GUM [genitourinary medicine] clinic is OK, but I have registered only as a civvy and not disclosed that I have done sex work. One issue is that they do not do oral swabs, even if you ask for them. So, if I do resume sex work to any degree, I will probably register under a pseudonym at a clinic in [another city].

[In terms of the Home Office report] Aside from the use of 'cis' raising my blood pressure, I found the report very fair and thorough.

My main issue is probably that to both official bodies and the public, sex work means street and/or trafficked workers. I wish the agencies would focus on tackling trafficking and prosecuting those guilty of it. It's also a concern that the Nordic model seems much more popular than decriminalisation. That said, I am guilty of not becoming involved in any campaigning about/advocacy for this, due to lack of time.

It would be great if independent escorts were seen as the real 'face' of sex work in the UK, but then I have to say, I think some women shoot themselves in the foot here, by e.g., not paying taxes, or doing bookings during lockdown. I don't think we can have our cake and eat it, too – if we want sex work to be seen as 'real' work then independent escorts need to behave like any other self-employed person. Hairdressers, driving instructors, nail technicians etc. couldn't work during the harsher lockdown periods, so why should sex workers feel they could? Working within the law would give any arguments for decriminalisation more weight, surely?

Likewise, I feel street workers have completely different issues, including addictions, that need to be tackled separately.

Beatrice's reflection (female professional dominatrix)

[Reading my first interview] reminded me that I have been in the industry a long time, but don't often take time to reflect on my sex work journey or how my relationship to sex work has changed. I started as a teenager and am now in my mid-thirties and it's been the only sustainable income I've had, but most of my peers are only aware of how I've worked in the last five years or so. Realising that I spent several years as a coerced young person is difficult to read, knowing it is my own story, but also a relief to realise how much I have changed and grown since then. I still need to be careful about unhealthy relationship dynamics in my personal life, but I am firmer now with the boundaries that I uphold when I am doing sex work.

In the last couple of years, I have largely wound up my sex work business despite facing the same running costs, due to the long lease I have on my sex work premises. This has severely impacted my financial situation, but I have in other ways been grateful to have taken a break from sex work. I've realised that I suffer with sexual trauma, and I certainly feel more embodied and present when I am performing sexual services less often.

It's interesting to read about my interaction with sex work pre-pandemic. Since then, the work has been far more scarce, and unreliable. Clients are no longer willing to pay deposits and are far more likely to cancel last minute or haggle on price and push for extra services that I do not offer.

The calibre of client is worse, particularly during lockdown as it's only the clients who are willing to bend/break the rules that are asking to see me. With those kinds of clients, I feel less likely to trust them if they tell me they have been isolating, won't use public transport to reach me or tell me that they have been vaccinated. I used to see middle aged and older clients who were mostly White, middle class, married professionals who were mostly respectful of my boundaries. When I have worked during COVID-19, that is no longer the case; I have attracted younger, less respectful, less educated, less wealthy men who make the work less comfortable (in addition to the added fears of catching or transmitting a deadly virus).

I've also conducted mostly one-on-one sessions, when I used to work with my sex work peers as often as possible. This is because clients are less willing to spend the money, and because I have been fearful of having more people in the booking due to COVID-19 (even if I know and trust my sex work colleague/s). Working one-on-one or working in a way where I do not have a friend waiting in another room or waiting nearby, due to trying to be more COVID-compliant, increases the dangers of sex work – as well as the feelings of isolation.

It's been particularly challenging offering charisma, warmth and sexual energy to a stranger in the middle of a pandemic, when I have felt totally alone myself with no social or romantic elements in my personal life to come home to. It's compounded by the fact that I'm not even attracted to men, and probably find them more repulsive than my straight sex worker friends. It's also been harder because there's fewer places to safely go after work, so it takes longer to wind down after a booking. Doing sex work during this period, even though it has been less often, has definitely been more challenging to my mental health. When thinking about friends, many of us have not missed doing sex work, and have only missed the money. Some of us have relied on old skills or learned new ones, and I suspect that not all of us will go back to doing sex work (although I know I will).

When thinking about the benefits of doing sex work, these do still apply. However, the scope of sex work as it is currently does not make it very inviting. If I was not already engaged in sex work, I probably wouldn't enter the industry right now or advise anyone else to do so.

Media coverage of sex work has improved recently, I think due to the public sympathies directed towards those who are now facing poverty due to relying on sex work during a global pandemic. Sex workers are also sick of being asked the same salacious questions about being poor by journalists, though. Sex work has become a much larger industry in the last year or two, due to swathes of people selling content online or signing up to offer webcam services. I don't know how much this has normalised sex work or reduced stigma, but I certainly hope it has to an extent. It has also meant that very experienced sex workers, such as myself, are called on even more to offer support to those entering the industry – despite the fact that we're often in more precarious positions with less access to conventional work.

I have been completely failed by the government's COVID-19 policy; as someone who was already claiming state benefits, I was not eligible for any boost in Universal Credit. I could not get any of the Self Employment Grants because of the little amount of money that I had made in previous years (due to having to be a full-time unpaid carer, and due to struggling with my own mental ill health).

Eventually I was able to obtain some funds from the local council due to having a business premises to do sex work, but even then, I knew I would only be able to get these funds by not being honest about the nature of the work that is conducted on the site. This fund from the council was used to pay my rent and was therefore given entirely to my landlord, who despite getting his full rent has been even worse about carrying out any essential repairs on the property. There is mould growing on the walls, the electricity stops working whenever there is heavy rain due to a regular leak, and there is limited light and ventilation due to it being a basement unit without any windows. I have built up my business over almost twenty years, and it is very sad to now be living on the breadline with so much money going to my landlord, for a property that I no longer use, and which is in such terrible condition.

I realise that this isn't strictly relevant to sex work, and that so many small businesses and self-employed people are struggling right now. But I leased this property to create a BDSM studio, as it is more illegal to set this up in a domestic premises (where I would at least have a short contract and have better chances of the property being properly maintained). The law makes it difficult to operate as a BDSM sex worker in any way that is above board, which in turn makes it difficult to claim any kind of financial support.

Bizarrely, despite all of the above, I actually feel more positive about the future than I did when I answered these questions before. That's because I've diversified my income and become less reliant on sex work. Even though my income is now much lower, I feel less tied to doing sex work and less tied to identifying myself as a sex worker first and foremost. I've felt more able to face my sexual trauma and seek therapy, due to the newfound clarity that I've derived by taking a long break from sex work for the first time. I've also felt more able to utilise my capabilities as a writer and a researcher, due to having extra time and motivation that I have acquired from taking a break from sex work. I am not sure how I will feel when I fully re-enter the industry, but I hope to maintain some sense of self awareness and curiosity when I do so.

[In relation to the Home Office report] I found the final report satisfying to read because of the open-ended nature of the questions, and the ways that the study properly acknowledged all aspects of the industry as well as the limits of the study itself. This mode of enquiry did lead to detailed, lengthy explanations rather than easily skimmable bullets and statistics – which does mean it may not be read as thoroughly and widely by some sex work advocates who do not have an academic background.

I felt that my quotes were used well, and I was glad to have contributed as I realise that, in many ways, I am not the 'typical' sex worker, so I felt I could add some extra points which may have otherwise been missed. I am pleased to have taken part in this instance as the study was designed well, however I am not always willing to engage with academic or government research. I don't trust many government bodies, and have found that in the past, some academic studies have not treated sex workers well.

I felt that this study was sensitive to my needs, and in part it was easier to engage due to having the space to write as opposed to share these often quite personal details in person. I am glad that the final report was so extensive, and that a book will also come out of this study to allow for even more detail.

I also hope that there will be some simple, accessible formats that make use of the information so that it can be utilised by sex work advocates, sympathetic journalists etc so that this study doesn't solely sit within an academic space. I am pleased to have been kept informed at all stages of the study, and to have been treated like a real and important part of the research process.

Helena's reflection (female independent escort and adult content provider)

I've changed my working practices quite a lot, initially in response to lockdown, but I will likely continue even after. I've worked hard on increasing my online earnings which should give me a useful passive income – always handy in times of illness or upheaval.

An astonishing number of sex workers stopped working during lockdown, which left the field wide open for those of us who continued. Prices have increased – not a huge amount, but there has been a general downward trend in recent years so this is a welcome reverse.

My previous business model was based on touring constantly and not working from home. With hotels shut, I had to resort to home working for the first time in several years. The place I was living, I had never intended to work from so I hadn't chosen it for discretion and ease of entry for clients. I tried to work there but clients found it too dodgy walking up and my neighbours had definitely noticed!

About a month into lockdown a friend called me: she was going crazy trying to work in her home city and suggested we share an apartment in [name of city], as she knew someone we could rent off. So, we headed for [name of city] and stayed about 8 weeks in total and were incredibly busy.

After this experience I was much keener to work in apartments going forward, and plan to continue in future. Having cooking and laundry facilities makes me feel much more 'off duty' at the end of the day, which is better for my work/life balance. Additionally, it means if I choose, I can bring someone with me as security, which makes me feel more confident to work later hours. (I usually finish at 8pm as after that time, the probability of someone turning up intoxicated rises significantly. I do make exceptions for regulars though.)

Going forward I intend to work from home around 75% of the time and just tour a few days per month.

As I've always declared my earnings and paid tax, I was able to claim the SEISS grants, along with the Business Interruption Loan. These have enabled me to invest in equipment and advertising to increase my online offerings.

Unfortunately, a lot of sex workers are not in such a fortunate position and there has been precious little help available – although some of the sex worker outreach organisations have tried their best with food voucher help and emergency grants. Also, one advertising site gave all sex workers free advertising during Lockdown 1, although you had to be coy and not mention any face-to-face services.

One thing to note is that although councils and police have told brothels and parlours to close and have force closed and fined some that tried to stay open clandestinely, they have completely ignored independent sex workers. I have only heard of one sex worker who was stopped and fined for breaking lockdown, and her client was fined, too.

[In terms of the Home Office report] Hmm. Mixed feelings. My overall impression is that the project had far too wide of an overview to actually provide any meaningful voices or data and I strongly (perhaps cynically) suspect that parts of it will be cherry-picked to support one political view or another, none of which will be of use or interest to people with actual lived experience of sex work.

I will say that after participating in several academic research projects into sex work, academia does at least make far more of an effort to include real sex workers' experience and opinions, in contrast to government-led projects which generally have a political or personal axe to grind.

Blake's reflection (non-binary independent escort and former sugar baby)

Reading back through my original interview, I mostly stand by everything I said. However, something that does stand out to me is a certain defensiveness – I think that I, and possibly a lot of sex workers, are very used to seeing a narrative of our work as tragedy and pathology, that makes us try to present it as, instead, something wholly positive. But the truth is, it's just a job. I was very happy as a sex worker, but I was also broke, because I fundamentally am not an organised or motivated enough person to make any kind of freelance work a good long term option. Not being able to talk openly about my job due to stigma was definitely an issue – there was always a certain balancing act between feeling like I shouldn't have to hide it and worry that being open could affect my career and education options in the future. Some clients were, honestly, the most boring men on the planet. It's just a job like any other, with good points and bad, that suits certain people more than others. It was something that I enjoyed for a time, but don't think I would want to do forever.

At the start of the first lockdown, I stopped doing sex work for the sake of social distancing. This was initially intended to be a temporary measure, but as time has gone on, I was forced by financial necessity to look into getting another job, and now I work in [social care]. I'm not sure whether I'll go back to sex work in the future. Originally, I wanted to, but it increasingly feels to me like something I've already done and an experience I've already had, and it's time to move on. This is kind of a weird feeling because while sex work is just a job, in a lot of ways it ends up feeling like a political identity as well, and I'm not really sure what my place is as an ex-sex worker to comment on policy etc. concerning sex work. Again, due to the stigma, sometimes it feels like there's half a decade of my life that I'm not allowed to talk about.

Discussion of second interviews

The pandemic inevitably affected participants financially and emotionally. The enforced distance from their work also enabled, as it has done for many people, reflection and re-evaluation of priorities. Cordelia had become involved in women's rights activism and was willing to listen to counter-views on the sex industry but use her own experience to offer what she felt was a pragmatic way forward:

> I think I will always feel that women should have the opportunity to enter sex work if they wish to do so, but it would be great if no one felt they had to. I am, for example, a big supporter of a universal basic income. (Female independent escort)

Beatrice appreciated the period of distance from sex work and the sex worker identity, not to reject that part of her life, but to spend time nurturing other pursuits and dimensions of selfhood, to address trauma and to find more balance overall, financially and personally. She plans to return to sex work, but with a new mindset. Blake found new work to get by and now feels that sex work is part of their past. Moving on however, is not easy when you cannot talk openly about your experience and particularly when you feel an emotional and political commitment to the sex work community: I pick up this issue in Chapter 5.

The reflections demonstrate differing views on whether and how people have continued to engage in sex work during the COVID-19 pandemic. As a scientist by training, and noting her own health vulnerabilities, Cordelia felt strongly about adherence to social distancing measures and lockdowns. She also expressed some exasperation that independent sex workers often call for their work to be treated as 'a job like any other', yet some did not respect the rules applied to other self-employed workers. While many sex workers were able to access self-employment income SEISS grants or business support loans, likely the majority did not have the right paperwork to demonstrate eligibility. Beatrice and Helena were able to access business support, but Beatrice describes how she had to lie about the nature of her business in order to rent premises. Other participants spoke about working from home in rented accommodation, which presents a similar issue.

Cordelia and Beatrice were generally happy with the Home Office report and liked that it captured a breadth of experiences. However, Beatrice notes that this was also a limitation given that the media, politicians and policymakers like to derive pithy observations or clear policy implications.

In addition, the academic style and length of the report mitigated against it being read in full beyond a small group of the most ardently interested. Similarly, Helena was concerned that in going for breadth, we had diluted the impact of the research. She feared that politicians and other readers would just 'cherry-pick' the quotes and insights, consistent with their pre-existing position.

Their reflections speak to the fraught business of doing academic research for the government. If government-commissioned researchers find that issues are complex and contradictory, they may not produce a report that is deemed 'useful' for policymaking. Indeed, their report might not get published at all (or slip out on the morning of an election announcement). The difficult position of criminology researchers in relation to the Home Office has been well documented (see Hope and Walters, 2008). Governments can commission research or open an inquiry to buy time. Should researchers continue to engage in government-commissioned research because of the (albeit fragile) promise of influencing policymaking? It is a significant gamble. On the one hand, that is exactly what impact-oriented academics want to do: make a difference. However, engaging the time and emotional energy of hundreds of participants over 1–2 years without then being able to point to policy change is difficult. It can affect both trust in academics and trust among the group researched. This in turn affects the prospects for conducting participative and inclusive research in the future.

Conclusion

While it is always difficult to be concrete on numbers when discussing the sex industry, female independent sex workers are a significant proportion of the overall group in England and Wales. I have used 'independent' here to refer to individuals who work for themselves. They include escorts, BDSM workers, webcammers, street workers, sugar babies and individuals producing adult content. Many of these women are working from home and using the internet and mobile phone to arrange meetings with, or marketing to, potential clients. Some actively choose the work; others choose in contexts of constraint (and the degrees of constraint vary widely); still others are groomed or coerced at some point and, even after escape, may continue to work either through choice, tired indifference or because of the barriers to accessing alternative work. It would be difficult, for example, to account to a future employer for the gaps in work record or for a conviction. Stigma and the threat of violence are challenges for female independent workers, particularly those who work mainly alone. Gender is implicated in how both are experienced. However, for those who are able to screen clients carefully and have the resources to implement safety measures, independent workers may not encounter violence over long periods of working. Indeed, they may be more at risk outside of work:

> I haven't been harmed at work, but I have been raped on a [dating app] date and on a night out, and in both of these cases I still didn't report precisely because I know that if I do, they will never take me seriously. Police don't take rape seriously at the best of times, but being a sex worker to them qualifies you as asking for it. (Female independent escort)

This leads to the final issue raised repeatedly by female independent workers: the legal context. Many argue that the current criminal law removes – and more prohibitionist legislation would further remove – the very mechanisms that could increase safety. These include working together; decriminalization; and access to online marketing platforms and screening tools. At the same, social policy support is needed to ensure, as Cordelia says, 'no one felt they had to' enter sex work.

4

Male Independent Sex Workers

Male workers are a smaller but still significant proportion of the sex industry. This applies in the UK and globally and includes here trans men and individuals designated male at birth who do not recognize a binary gender identity but may advertise as male (again, for more on the experiences of trans individuals and non-binary people selling sex, see: Brown et al, 2010; D'Ippoliti and Botti, 2017; Samudzi, 2017; Nuttbrock and Bockting, 2018; Van Schuylenbergh et al, 2018; Orchard et al, 2020). Research suggests that the majority of male sex workers sell sex to other men, but some sell sex to women or couples. The gender of clients is not necessarily linked to personal sexual orientation (Baral et al, 2015).

In the Home Office study, we spoke to an organization working with men engaged in sex work and they were keen to stress that '[s]ome men who exchange sexual or intimate acts for monetary or other benefit, particularly on the gay street scene, may embrace, repudiate or be ambivalent towards notions of "sex work" and the identity of "sex worker", depending on the context' (Hester et al, 2019, p 11). Morris (2018, np) uses the term 'incidental sex work' to describe 'forms of casual, occasional, unsolicited commercial sex, arranged between gay, bisexual, and queer men on social media platforms such as Grindr'. This in turn emerges from a particular historic context of criminalization and stigmatization of gay men in Britain and elsewhere, who consequently evolved spaces and places where men could meet for company and for sex. Indeed, Crofts (2014, p 181, drawing on Weeks, 1981) says that: 'Male-to-male sex work has not been regarded as a distinct regulatory issue because historically it has been fundamentally intertwined with the regulation and legal framing of male homosexuality.' It is argued that there was effectively a conflation between male sex work and gay sexual conduct (Logan, 2017). Male sex workers were able to 'blend into' the gay scene (Crofts, 2014, p 181, drawing on Whowell, 2010) and evaded feminist concern and scrutiny because 'the great majority of activity' took place 'between men'. Male sex workers providing services to female clients is almost entirely off the British regulatory and academic radar (Kingston et al, 2020, are a notable exception), since this activity tends to be arranged privately, one-on-one, and numbers overall are small. A small number of male workers providing services to women did participate in the original Home Office survey and in the email interviews.

Like female independent sex workers, male independent workers are using the internet to arrange meetings with clients, either through adult services websites, social media profiles or personal websites. Male workers selling to men were more likely in interviews to mention meetings arranged through dating apps or non-sex-work listings sites, which fits with Morris' (2018) description of 'incidental' encounters. Sanders and colleagues (2021) note also that 'male sex workers are less likely to report crimes to the police and less likely to utilize sex worker forums than female sex workers'. This more 'isolated' way of working is borne out to some extent in the interviews.

While this chapter recognizes and explores the differences in practice and context between male and female independent workers, it also identifies common ground in perceptions of the benefits and challenges of sex working, hopes for change in the sex industry and future aspirations.

Participant narratives (original email interview)

In this section are presented two short summaries from Edmund (a male former adult film actor) and Fabian (a male independent BDSM worker). In both cases, the shorter format is used because their original email interview responses were more concise, and less adaptable to presenting as a story, than the others. Following these are presented longer narratives from Hector (an independent escort and erotic masseur); Sebastian (an independent escort and erotic masseur); and Fenton (an independent escort, adult film actor and sexual health activist). The excerpts are followed by discussion, drawing in also brief quotes from experiences from other participants who gave first interviews in the original research.

Edmund's story (male former adult film actor)

I got asked to work on a BDSM porn shoot in a technical capacity, setting up and directing green screen shots for web content. Then I got asked if I'd do any in front of camera work. It was only a one-time thing. I'd do it again if the opportunity arose though. I was paid by order/invoice through the director's production company. [This was useful because it was] at a time where contracts in my regular job were quite sparse for me, due to not having much experience. My primary partner and I (we're both polyamorous) are fluid bonded (i.e., we use protection for sex with others but not between us) and the shoot was without protection, as is usually the case in porn, it seems, so [my partner and I] had to have a discussion around that. And I obviously had to get fully checked for STIs beforehand and had to get a signed form stating I was clear. I get checked every 3–6 months as a matter of course anyway. I don't plan on doing more adult work but it's certainly something I'd do again. I half joke about going into the porn industry when I retire.

Fabian's story (male independent BDSM worker)

[I got started in sex work, specialising in kink and BDSM] when I first moved to [city] to start my university course. A student grant was not enough so I needed another income. I worked around my studies [and] at the moment I see clients whenever I am able to. The people who see me all identify as female (regardless of what genitals they were assigned in the womb). The biggest challenge is finding reliable clients. Risks are numerous which can never be eliminated but can be minimised and managed. This applies to both myself and the client, which is why I insist on thorough negotiations before doing anything intimate. [My future plans are to] continue saving money to purchase a property and to secure a retirement fund. I'll also continue to support the communities that I am a part of.

Hector's story (male independent escort and erotic masseur)

I first started after a one-night stand offered me money. I accepted. I then started selling sex part-time and after a few years became a full-time erotic masseur.

Initially I combined sex work with my full-time profession, working two or three nights a week. Gradually I was earning more through sex work, and it gave me more time to myself so eventually, I became a full-time sex worker. I have half retired now, but still see a few regulars.

I worked as self-employed and I worked through escort agencies, but not for long. Mostly, I worked alone from my own home. I used local hard copy press when you were still able but then almost exclusively online from my own website and through a variety of advertising sites.

Clients would call. I would vet them as much as possible, checking their phone numbers online, through social media. If I was visiting them, I would check they were at a hotel or, if possible, get a home number for a home visit. Most however visited me. I would arrange for them to park near the house, call, so that I could check they were where they said they were, then direct them in. Most appointments were for an hour/ half hour.

[Can you describe your clients?] So varied. Not one demographic although I suppose most were fairly middle class. When I escorted in [name of city], I saw wealthy Arabs and Chinese who would tip a thousand pounds and with erotic massage, plumbers who gave me a £10 tip.

Their reasons for booking were varied. Some were lonely, some just horny, some were experimenting with their sexuality. I saw a lot of clients who were disabled and a lot of elderly clients. A lot of couples wanted to try something different. Many clients wanted to experiment sexually and, for whatever reason, couldn't at home. There is, or was, no set type or reason. As a sex worker I offered a service to the public and the public are a varied lot of people. It was the constant excitement which I think made sex work so fascinating.

When I started, I was an escort. That usually involved for me longer appointments, often overnights. That was more stressful work because it required more of an act. Being nice to someone for 12 hours, or on occasion two or three days, is hard work. It's like being a personal servant, in that you are in their company and trying to entertain for a long period of time. You often had to have a lot of sexual stamina as well, but that depended on the client.

As I become older (I worked for almost 17 years), I moved onto erotic massage. The work was easier and less stressful, if a little less exciting. […]

You have to be open-minded and willing to accommodate a variety of people from different backgrounds and experiences. You may meet a Duke one day and a scaffolder the next. I don't think that you have to be a people person, but certainly, you must be a calm and versatile person in that you have to meet challenges with an even temperament.

I sometimes shared premises with others. It made me feel safer and cut costs. You constantly feared being raided by the police or being reported so I was always careful, and you were constantly moving. [So] it became easier just to work alone from my own home. It made life lonely sometimes, but the law sadly treats sex workers like criminals and it's wrong to do so when we are simply offering a service to consenting adults.

You work alone because of the law, and you never know who you will meet. I only ever saw two violent clients in 17 years. I was able to deal with them, but some sex workers have not been so lucky. The law is responsible for this – not clients and not sex workers. […]

On a very personal level I had to deal with the constant fear of others' opinion of my work. I'm quite a strong person however, and quite insular, so as long as I was positive about my work and my life, then I kept myself to myself. I was lucky in that I had a profession which

I used as a cover for my lifestyle when necessary. Others were not that lucky and often invented another job. Having to hide your work because of stigma is perhaps the worst aspect of being a sex worker.

[My future plans are to] carry on seeing regulars and enjoy life. I've been sensible with the money I earned and who knows exactly what the future will bring. No one does.

Sebastian's story (male independent escort and erotic masseur)

Escorting was always something I was interested in trying, I can't really say exactly why. Looking at some of the answers I've given to the later questions – particularly thinking about getting to explore my own sexuality and other men's – probably goes some way to me figuring that out.

I take 11 years ago as my 'official' start as that was when I made a concerted effort to find work, that is, I created several free escort profiles online on hook-up sites. […] During the two years prior to 'officially' starting, I had a couple of paid meets. These were quite random occurrences. I had a (non-escort) profile on a hook-up site on which I said I was open to being paid for work. I picked up a couple of jobs from that (one of which was wallpaper stripping and decorating, with sex afterwards). My very first paid meet was from answering an advert on [listing site] from a guy looking for a life model – I was fully ready for him not to actually be looking for a life model, and sure enough after 10 minutes of sketching, he asked if I wanted to watch some porn and things progressed (briefly) from there. […]

I don't have another job (another income source), but I don't see loads of clients. I don't think clients like to think that I'm seeing a lot of other clients, that they are just one in a long line, although some clients like to hear details of what I get up to on other appointments. On average I see anything from 1–5 clients a week, but it varies.

Appointments are organised by phone. Sometimes initially organised by email, or by messages online, but any appointments with new clients will be finalised over the phone, with a call from them to me, on a number that's not withheld. I prefer to speak to someone beforehand if I'm meeting them for the first time, even just for a short chat, as I can get a better feel for them that way and it also helps weed out the timewasters (guys that just want to email or text about meeting up, wanting to know what would happen during an appointment, who get off on doing only that with no intention of ever actually meeting). […] I see exchanging phone numbers as a small act of trust and commitment. […]

I'm paid in cash, usually at the end of an appointment, occasionally at the beginning. I have on occasion been paid online (like, through [name of online payment system]) and once by cheque from a client I knew well, but these are the exceptions; I much prefer cash in hand. There's no-one else involved.

[A]ll my clients are male. There's a wide age range, from 18 to late 70s, though I'd say the majority of my clients are in their 40s or 50s. The majority are White British. [...]

In terms of my living/working arrangements, I live with my partner, who isn't involved in the sex industry. I do in-calls (clients come to me) when he's not in.

It's difficult to generalise about the other escorts and masseurs I know and that I've worked with. I will say though, my work is very 'male-focused'. [...] With the other sex workers I know, some are doing the job as their sole means of income, others are using money from sex work to supplement other jobs. The ones I know tend to be a bit older, in their 30s–50s (I'm in my 40s). With this question, the person that springs to mind is a friend who is an escort specialising in cross-dressing meets. We actually met when he was looking for another escort for a duo appointment, and after a few more appointments together, we started meeting up socially for tea and cheap theatre tickets. He would very much like to leave escorting and managed it for a few months when he got a job [outside of sex work]. However, with the wages being what they are and an increase in his rent and personal issues with his family, he's had to start seeing some of his previous regular clients again, though he's managed to limit it to one a week. [...]

A good session [is where a client] leaves happier than when they arrived. It's not just physical, though physical should definitely not be underestimated. Even if all that was gained from a good session was 'just physical' that would still be something great. There are or can be emotional and psychological benefits. Something as simple as giving over the time to explore and enjoy your own body, and have someone explore and enjoy it at the same time.

In terms of challenges, keeping on top of sexual health can be challenging sometimes. The clinic that I regularly attended for 7 years, the Working Men's Project, based at St Mary's in Paddington (London), lost its funding just under two years ago and closed down. The Project was a sexual health service specifically for men working in the sex industry and I had a really strong and consistent relationship with the two nurse practitioners who ran the clinic. I don't think I fully appreciated at the time how much I relied on the Working Men's Project when it came to my sexual health. I mean, I'm a fully grown responsible man, I'm on PrEP, I get checked regularly, I know where I can go to do that, but the Working Men's Project gave me a focal point, staff that I trusted who I knew I could contact if I had any problems and who understood the job I was doing. The Project's closure is still a keenly felt loss to me.

After it lost its funding, The Working Men's Project, along with its sister service, The Praed Street Project (a service specifically for women in the sex industry), which also lost its funding, were briefly amalgamated into something called 'Projects@Mary's'. This offered a less comprehensive (more reactive, less holistic) clinic for male, female and trans sex workers, but that too lost its funding after a year.

I've never felt myself to be in any physical danger during the course of my work. There can be clients who are quite emotionally demanding. Again, I've never felt at any risk, but it does make me aware that some clients rely on and invest a lot personally into our sessions and I have to be careful to navigate that. I mean, these are fleeting moments in men's lives, I don't want to make it sound grander than it is, but those moments can be intense and meaningful and carry a weight.

The only other thing that springs to mind when thinking about this question [about harms, risks and challenges] is my family, who don't know what I do for a living. I live some distance from them and in some ways I'm quite separate from them, but I visit often and generally have to fudge or give non-answers to questions about how I'm making money. Being in a civil partnership does offer a certain amount of cover and I'm pretty sure they have some inkling of what I get up to, but it's never been explicitly stated. I'd quite like them to know, but I don't necessarily want to be the one to tell them. It sometimes feels like I'm denying them access not just to me, but to all the experiences I've had and all the things I've learnt. Of course, not all experiences and not all things learnt during the course of sex work would be shareable with my mum and dad, but it's a whole different way of life, a different way of seeing the world, that I'm holding back from them.

[What changes have you seen over time?] One of the biggest changes, I'm pretty sure for quite a lot of male sex workers and clients as well, is the availability of PrEP (I don't know if female sex workers or straight male sex workers have felt its impact with the same force, possibly trans workers have, I'm not sure). I know PrEP has much wider implications beyond sex work, but the removal of the fear of HIV can't be underestimated, especially for gay and bisexual men. I don't think I fully grasped how heavily HIV weighed on my mind until I stepped out from under it. [...]

Maybe it's not changed, maybe it's just that I've been paying more attention, but the public debate around sex work seems more hostile (to sex workers) recently. Maybe it's the increased debate about the Nordic model, the people who are pushing for that. I guess it's nothing new to paint all sex workers as victims; to paint all sex workers as female, all clients as predatory, abusive men. But the threat of the Nordic model and the damage it could do feels new and very real.

You'll probably already be aware of the study, but I'd want to draw your attention to Internet Sex Work: Beyond the Gaze by Sanders et al. On two separate occasions, during radio interviews/debates, I've heard MPs involved with committees on sex work dismiss the study. [One said] that the study didn't look into brothels, which is what the committee she was involved in was specifically looking at. That would be understandable if the committee didn't then go on to make recommendations regarding websites and online advertising!

I'm not entirely sure what my future plans are. Things feel a little in flux at the moment.

Fenton's story (male independent escort, actor and sexual health activist)

[I got started] five years ago. I had a partner who had severe depression and a criminal record from an offence of cruising […] all meaning he could not keep down a job and struggled getting to meetings for benefits. He needed a home-visit therapist so on top of my part-time job (the only one I was able to get), I started escorting (with his permission).

I see three clients a month currently: three a week in the past. Sometimes more, sometimes less. I take other work also like public speaking at welfare events. I combine a lot of my sex work with sexual health activism and support for NHS needs e.g., creating adult films that encourage people to consider PrEP as a form of HIV prevention. […]

[I advertise] mainly online but my regulars have my number and message me. Some will email me after exploring online content. Male sex workers rarely use the buddy system (telling a friend where you are and who the client is during a session; calling the buddy in front of the client and saying you will call them back in x amount of time after the session) as clients might also be worried that them being gay gets out, so the paranoia can be high.

I take a deposit covering the additional travel costs of an outcall. I do that via a business account bank transfer. The rest, including total for in-calls, are paid in cash. I always accept the money upfront and never leave the money in the bedroom while in the loo/other room. I bank transfer for overnight clients as you can't guard money when you are asleep. If a cost is more money than a client's withdrawal amounts a day, then I do a bank transfer. Never bank transfer to my own personal account as the birth name appears to the client that way. I make the business name very discreet.

Most of my clients are recovering from the 'chem sex' scene, meaning they have gotten so used to sex on drugs that they are afraid they cannot enjoy sober sex. I work with them to see sexual tension and awkwardness as part of the challenge that adds value to the experience, making it more real and an experience that can be remembered.

Another set of my clients are disabled or have Intellectual Learning Differences and, as a result, they are often treated as asexual or undesirable. I help them discover a sex life that they are equally entitled to, giving them confidence for finding a partner they can share it with in future.

Some of my clients are living a double life, pretending to be straight. I give them as much genuine chemistry/romance as I can because I want them to know after a difficult patch of accepting their sexuality, there is a bright future after it: sharing a life with someone they romantically and truly sexually love. Some people are in arrangements where each partner knows it happens. […]

Most people start escorting when they need money. I did. However, I also started because I needed to step beyond my comfort zones in my sex life, because performance anxiety was impacting my personal sex life initially. I also had a dependent that needed my care.

[In terms of the benefits of my work] I am happy. My partner and I do not see sex as the only thing important in a relationship and are unthreatened by each other's sex life with third parties. [We focus on] cherishing companionship, understanding and the whole person, more than primarily sex.

I am doing well and harnessing my sex work helped me. […] Even as a Male Sex Worker we are a minority within a minority as we don't have an established voice on our vulnerabilities. Vulnerabilities like sex workers caught up in the 'chem-sex' scene [which has become] so popular in the gay community, for medicating the trauma of growing up rejected in a Hetero-centralised world. Or police not seeing violence because it just looks like another case of a gay man overdosing on drugs used in chem sex.

Before sex work, I was so desperately poor and incapable of pleading to family for support. I struggled to take care of my ex-partner. Through sex work, I afforded the therapeutic care he needed and gave him a stable life. Then we realised we had no longer become romantically attached, but rather linked through a carer/cared-for relationship, and we decided to move forward in our lives, so each became more independent.

A challenge [of sex work] is that if I were in trouble, I would not contact police for help. I cannot trust them. They are like a formal decoration on society: one that may help other people, so has value.

If I had a seizure (I have epilepsy) with a client, as most clients think escorting or being a client is illegal [...] they are unlikely to call 999 in case they get arrested or the event outs them, breaking their double life with a wife.

Sex work for men is dangerous currently. Many escorts get high with clients, meaning they are vulnerable to robbery, rape and attack regardless of muscle mass. Sex workers can be attacked by homophobes or as my friend was: thrown out a moving car because they assumed (correctly) he was living with HIV. [...]

[In terms of my future plans], sex workers need equal rights so fighting for that will not stop till it happens. With equal rights it also means that, landing a follow-on job (if I decided to change), would become a more attractive offer as work could not be taken away from me by a boss, or news story, not liking my job history.

Discussion of first interviews

Reasons for entry into the sex industry for male participants varied from economic need, caring responsibilities, sexual self-exploration, incidental events – or a combination. The incidental encounters (Morris, 2018) – Sebastian gives the example of responding to an ordinary advert for a decorator, which led to sex – were not evident in the accounts of female sex workers who participated in the study, though may happen. One participant highlighted how, as a new migrant, sex work provided an easier way to earn money:

I had period where sex work was my main job, others where I also worked in café, restaurants, cinema etc. As migrant with limited English, I didn't have a lot of options, but sex work paid better and gave more freedom than other jobs. (Male erotic masseur)

Fenton's comment in parentheses, 'with his permission', raises the question of how sex workers negotiate their work with partners:

[My partner] needed a home-visit therapist so on top of my part-time job (the only one I was able to get) I started escorting (with his permission).

Similarly, this female independent escort positioned her work as a mutual agreement between her and her partner to address their financial difficulties:

I worked solely alone. I arranged all meets while my husband was at work. He was aware I made the decision to be an escort and was supportive of the decision (it was made together due to our financial constraints). (Female former independent escort)

Edmund too described discussing with his main partner, with whom he is fluid-bonded, the implications of taking part in a pornography shoot, where actors did not use protection. Participants in the wider study, male and female, talked of partners helping out with their business (for example, with IT); while others found that sex work made personal intimate relationships difficult or impossible.

Financial freedom and flexibility were the key benefits noted by male independent sex workers. Others spoke of confidence-building – Fenton had spoken at the United Nations about HIV activism within the pornography industry – and of being able to afford time to volunteer:

The money helps a lot in keeping me in good physical and mental health, and also gives me the privilege of finding the time to do a lot of community work. (Fabian, male independent BDSM worker)

Like the female workers in the previous chapter, male participants also spoke of the emotional satisfaction of doing work that they could see made people happy. This included sexual satisfaction but also meeting clients' need for connection and being authentic. This was not necessarily a feature of all client meetings, but occurred sufficiently for participants to recall those moments in a way that confirmed for them that their work had a therapeutic and socially important function:

I know it is cliché, but sex work can also be beautiful. Holding someone you don't know in your arms as they cry because they have never been held by another man is beautiful. Most of the time (after doing this for 15 years) sex work is just boring like another work, but there are/were moments of true of connections with clients and I think that many clients' emotional, sexual and physical – and for some spiritual – health have improved because of the time spent with me (or the thousands of other sex workers). We keep speaking about an epidemic of loneliness. We, sex workers, are at the frontline of this epidemic. Although it is completely unrecognised, our work really helps many people. (Male erotic masseur)

Most commonly, male workers identified physical safety, stigmatization and sexual health as key risks of their work. An issue specifically mentioned by participants in relation to the male sex work scene – although drug use and sex work do overlap in other areas of the sex industry – is 'chem sex', the use of 'drugs (such as crystal methamphetamine, GHB (gamma hydroxybutyrate) or mephedrone, also known as "miaow miaow") that enhance sex and make individuals feel uninhibited' (Hester et al, 2019, p 19). Participants talked of the risks to both workers and clients getting high: the possibility of overdose, of assault or robbery. As part of his campaigning and awareness approach, Fenton specifically offers 'sober sex' as a service to men who have been so immersed in chem sex that they feel unable to perform or feel anything without using drugs. Male participants also noted the closure of, or increasingly limited access to, sexual health services, an issue also raised by Cordelia in Chapter 3. Their experience speaks to the ripple effect and often unseen harms of austerity after 2008, which saw the closure of countless services and specialist projects for different groups in society. Access is also a challenge for those working in rural areas or small towns, often requiring travel to cities to access support (see Scott et al, 2006).

Finding reliable clients, who were safe and genuine, was another issue and, related to this, irregularity of income could be a problem. Like female sex workers, a number of participants cited the prevailing legal framework as increasing risk because they felt unable to report assault or harassment:

> I had moments where I was afraid for my safety: I was insulted and threatened, and I knew that in these cases I wouldn't report to the police. And the aggressor knew it too. (Male erotic masseur)

Participants in this study worked alone most of the time. Hector had tried working with others from a premises but found the advantages of safety and cost-saving did not compensate the stress of potential police raids. Working on duo appointments (two sex workers, one client) could however be a way of meeting colleagues and making friends, as in other workplaces. Socializing with other sex workers was described as important to 'let off steam' about the work, but also, for those working in secrecy, a chance to relax without the need for constant self-vigilance in conversation.

It was noted in the opening of this chapter that men selling *exclusively* to women appears to be a smaller proportion of the male sex worker population overall. In the Home Office study, only two out of 500+ participants who responded to the survey identified as being in this category, both of whom were BDSM workers, although other male workers had seen single women or couples occasionally. Fabian describes his clients as follows:

> On the whole, the social class has been middle (lower and upper), and majority Caucasian women between 20–45 years old. Occupations have ranged from school heads, medical doctors, university academics, members of parliament, television actors, and artists. The main

motivation has been the need for a non-judgemental, confident, fully negotiated service where the woman can experience some escapism (or stress relief) within a safer space. (Fabian, male independent BDSM worker)

From the data in this study therefore, it is White women with economic and professional privilege who are both able to pay and to conceive of paying, counter to prevailing gender-power relations and expectations. The decision to pay may also link to the services sought, which are specialist.

Among the male participants, there was universal support for decriminalization of sex workers and clients. Many expressed concerns over the tenor and temperature of the public debate on the sex industry and, as they saw it, the hypocrisy and unwillingness to recognize the diverse and lived experiences of sex workers. Sebastian develops this in the second interview in this chapter and, elsewhere in the data, Edmund describes how:

I attended the protest outside Westminster against the Trump-inspired 'anti-trafficking' law – in the US known as SESTA/FOSTA [Fight Online Sex Trafficking Act/Stop Enabling Sex Traffickers Act] and talked to a pro Domme [professional dominatrix] friend there. She was concerned that it would endanger lives of sex workers [...] and made mention of the hypocrisy of ministers looking at passing this into law when a number of them were/are clients of hers. (Edmund, male former adult film actor)

Fenton stressed the importance of education and awareness raising following decriminalization. He felt that this would send a public signal about sex workers which could help reduce stigma and put clients on alert that violent or discriminatory behaviour was not acceptable and would be reported. Hector criticized current UK laws as a 'nightmare' and dangerous. He argued that:

[W]e need to allow up to 4 sex workers to share premises for safety and companionship. We need to stop the brothel raids and concentrate resources on that handful of sex workers who do need help, either because of social deprivation or having been coerced. We need to recognise sex workers as self-employed business people and allow them to access ordinary banking and commercial services just like any other self-employed person. (Hector, male independent escort and erotic masseur)

Having been privy to the full dataset as a researcher, it was interesting how different sex workers describe the industry as a whole. Hector described the proportion of sex workers who are coerced or engaged in survival sex as a 'handful'. At one stakeholder meeting I had during the data collection phase, the participants were bemused when I said that some who had responded to our survey described sex work as a chosen career. They felt that sex work was invariably an outcome of economic constraint, social inequalities and punitive welfare and migrant regimes. It reminded me that all of us – whether researchers or researched – rarely have a complete picture of social life and will often rely on what we know, and *look for what we know*, from our own contexts, contacts and beliefs.

In terms of future plans, Fenton, Fabian and one other participant mentioned continuing to engage in sex work and health activism, as well as community work. Hector was planning to largely retire having been 'sensible with the money I earned', although continue to see a few regulars. Another participant noted that his work forced him to eat well, go to the gym and drink alcohol rarely and that he would work for the 'next 10 years, maybe' (male erotic masseur).

Participant reflections (second email interview)

This section presents second interviews with Edmund, Fabian, Sebastian and Fenton conducted in spring 2021. First and second interviews for all but Hector appear in this chapter, who did not do a second interview.

Edmund's reflection (male former adult film actor)

On reflection it all still stands. I haven't changed my view on it at all. [Acting in a pornographic film] was a very positive experience. But then, as a financially sound, White, middle class, heteroflexible cis male who chose to engage in it for the experience: I'm in a very privileged position.

Fabian's reflection (male independent BDSM worker)

It feels slightly strange reading back on the answers I gave, despite it not being that long ago. I think some of my language has changed. If I were to answer the questions again then some of the wording would be different, and I'd go into more detail, though the overall gist would remain the same. My feelings and experience are still aligned from when I submitted those answers to you.

I'd go into more detail with question 11 – 'What are the (a) challenges (b) risks (c) harms of what you do (did)?' [see Appendix 4 of Hester et al, 2019] as I feel my answer was lacking. Challenges would be first finding clients, then developing a good working relationship with them to improve the chances of repeat customers. Getting paid can also be challenging, I've been lucky in this regard as no one so far has tried to withhold payment, however many other women sex workers I know have issues with new clients refusing to pay.

The risks we can be vulnerable to are, again, problems with payment, clients behaving inappropriately or violently, and a lack of societal support when we really need it (in my experience the police often lack sympathy / empathy when reporting crimes such as theft or sexual assault, and we don't have the laws / legal interpretation needed to support the sex industry).

I'd also emphasise the fact that being an able bodied cis het male sex worker still gives me a significant higher privilege than that of my female / LGBTQ+ / disabled colleagues who would usually have a very different experience to me, with increased levels of risk to themselves.

The COVID-19 pandemic has meant I've not had any sex work since the first lockdown in March 2020, which has led to a severe financial crisis in my life. My income was also affected when the high-profile London fetish clubs I work in were forced to close. I have been approached by clients for sessions during this time however I did not deem it safe enough due to the highly transmissible nature of the virus, along with uncertainties about the variants. Wearing a face mask while being intimate with clients sounds like an unacceptably high level of risk to me, I have not been able to think of a safe way of conducting sessions in person. While I don't have any serious underlying medical conditions, I have been offering support to people who are vulnerable and shielding, and I would not want them to become sick because of what I may have been exposed to.

Protections for sex workers have been almost non-existent unless the worker is registered as self-employed and has the financial records to make a claim valid. We can get Universal Credit if we have the relevant paperwork like identification and proof of address, though this provides the bare minimum to live on, if that.

This just emphasises even more to me the importance of having sex work recognised as legitimate work, and the legal protections that come with it.

It felt positive to be included in this study, and I appreciated in particular the section on BDSM as it didn't come across as sensationalised or subject to a 'moral panic'. This is definitely one of the better reports I have read, but I still believe more outreach is needed, and government support, to help destigmatise an industry that has been persecuted throughout history.

Sebastian's reflection (male erotic masseur and independent escort)

Reading back, I was surprised how much I wrote. There's a bit of a fashion for tell-all escort memoirs; seems I filled in those follow-up questions in lieu of writing mine.

Work pretty much fell off a cliff at the beginning of the first lockdown: I had an appointment with a client on Wednesday March 19th then didn't meet any clients again until May 19th, when myself and a regular client both happened to be in town for 'legitimate' reasons, so we doubled that up with an appointment in a room I hired. Then I didn't start properly seeing clients again until mid-June, with the work becoming steadier and continuing fairly evenly, though at a reduced rate to that of pre-lockdown, until mid-December, when the work fell right away again. With the third lockdown and news coverage of the variants, stayed like that until I started seeing two regulars again towards the end of January and throughout February; and it's only now, coming up to the middle of March [2021], that I'm starting to book appointments with other clients again.

After the definiteness of lockdown was over, that reduced work rate I mentioned was partly down to circumstance, partly down to choice: I'm not able to offer in-calls as easily because my partner is around more; some clients' daily routines, ability to host, and travel plans are still disrupted; even outwith that, there's still a fear and hesitancy from some clients about meeting; and there's a hesitancy on my part as well, about taking on too many appointments, particularly in too short a space of time (I would prefer that appointments were spaced out a bit more).

With not being able to host easily: on the one hand, it would be nice to get back to a routine and know that I can easily see clients in my own space again, but on the other, when I'm still wanting to take things slow, it's been good to have that excuse, to have something definite to point to when saying that I can't meet.

I'm in a reasonably secure financial position, in that I live with my partner who's retired, and I've so far been eligible for and taken the three grants available through the Self-Employment Income Support Scheme (SEISS). I can't help being concerned about what the future will bring in terms of work and if things will remain as secure as they are, but I know how lucky I am compared to some of the working guys I know.

During the pandemic, I would sometimes see how other countries were responding specifically to (in-person) sex workers. And I was sort of torn between wanting specific guidance from the government and wanting to be left to make my own judgement calls. What I do, what I offer, is never going to be COVID-secure, even in the loosest meaning of that term, and I guess if that doesn't get acknowledged by the guidelines, if what I do and what I offer isn't acknowledged, then I am left to make up my own mind about when and how I start seeing clients again. I can sort of keep an eye on the guidance for 'personal services' (hairdressers, 'regular' masseurs, etc), but that still doesn't really cut it, and there are loopholes (or flex) in that category anyway – I've been getting a sports massage monthly since July [2020]. Maybe I should have treated myself like a nightclub or live music, just stopped completely, but was that necessary or viable?

It was difficult enough trying to navigate all that with a degree of financial security; I can't imagine what it would have been like without.

My experience of participating in the study has been very positive.

I guess when I read the final report, my take-away observation was pretty simple: it's that it's all there, all the variety and breadth of sex work, all the ways it exists, the good and the bad of it, the sometimes funny, often times complicated nature of it. And while I feel good about what the report has captured, I feel at the same time maybe a little sceptical, find it hard to believe that what the report shows will make its way into the general debate about sex work. That's in no way the fault of the report. It just sometimes feels that trying to shift from that single-minded view of sex work towards something that better reflects what's in the report, that feels like a mammoth task.

There was a feature on COVID-19 and sex work on Woman's Hour back in [2020]. Of course, I was interested to hear it and they announced the participants at the start of the feature, first [a spokesperson] from The English Collective of Prostitutes and then secondly, [a journalist]. And as soon as that second guest was announced, I knew it wouldn't be a debate about sex work during the COVID pandemic, it would be just another debate about sex work itself. I tried to give the programme the benefit of the doubt, that maybe [the journalist] was there to provide balance, but really, balance to what?

The feature and the way it was handled seemed almost emblematic of the general debate about sex work – a sex worker wanting to talk about the practicalities and difficulties of their job and the needs they have, instead having to debate their right to exist, being met with suspicion and the diminishing of their lived experience, constantly having to push for their voice to be placed at the centre of a discussion about their work.

Fenton's reflection (male independent escort, adult film actor and sexual health activist)

COVID-19 was hard on all of us. Fewer clients wanted to hire sex workers. [...] The financial support from government was not suited to sex workers, who often are without a tax history or reliable bank accounts [...] and yet even with these extra hardships, rent needed paying and bills paying. [...] Those wishing to attack a sex worker are not deterred by it breaking the law to hire one. It is only seen as further justification for attacking the sex worker.

[In terms of how I feel in relation to the Home Office report], the sex worker community classically feels used after academic research. As used as the exploitation the research often states it aims to end. Why is this? Well, the emotional and intellectual labour of the sex worker is undervalued and often unpaid (justified as to avoid bias) and yet the researchers are paid to present the sex workers' experiences, like a colonialist prospecting in other nations for what can be sold.

With this particular piece of work, I was happy with the testimonies included by sex workers: they were powerful. But I know the general statements used elsewhere could be used by the communities who are dead set to undermine the rights of sex workers. Even stating how many sex workers there are in the UK can be taken away from a research paper context and weaponised by those willing to do so for other aims. Aims such as seeing sex workers as collateral damage to an experiment in sex work prohibitionism, to study its effects on sexism in society, or those motivated by religious doctrine.

Since this research was completed, I've seen the sex worker community move more and more to a position of being unable to trust any organisations which are not outright supporting the full decriminalisation of sex work. [...] This 'pass or fail question' [...] will be a trust filter for any organisations hoping to have productive sex worker engagement and outreach in the future.

Discussion of second interviews

In general, participants felt that what they wrote first time still stood, although the experience of re-reading was revealing:

It feels slightly strange reading back on the answers I gave, despite it not being that long ago. I think some of my language has changed. (Fabian, male independent BDSM worker)

Reading back, I was surprised how much I wrote. (Sebastian, male erotic masseur and independent escort)

Fabian reflects that he would have given more detail on harms and risks and in his second interview mentions negative experiences with the police.

Sebastian explains how he has switched into new platforms, including Twitter, which took time to orient to, 'wading into this unknown marketplace'. In part this relates to changing policies among online adult content providers who are likely anticipating where government legislation will move next. Fenton describes problematic elements in the Audiovisual Media Services Regulations being dropped in 2020 but that he fears they will re-emerge in future legislation, such as the awaited Online Harms Bill.

For all participants, COVID-19 has brought significant challenges. Fabian describes a 'severe financial crisis' but cannot see how he can continue to work safely. An active volunteer in his community, he says:

> While I don't have any serious underlying medical conditions, I have been offering support to people who are vulnerable and shielding, and I would not want them to become sick because of what I may have been exposed to. (Fabian, male independent BDSM worker)

The experience had clarified further for him the precarious existence of sex workers and the urgent need for law reform and concomitant protections. For Sebastian, as we emerge from the pandemic, the transition has given him a reason to take the return to work at his own pace.

Fenton argues that the experience of lockdown has shown what would happen under Nordic model conditions: many sex workers were continuing to work 'underground' due to financial constraint and were, nationally and globally, subject to higher levels of violence and harm. Sebastian describes the situation of two friends, one a current sex worker and one a former sex worker:

> [Current sex worker] has had to access the hardship fund set up by the SWARM [Sex Work Advocacy and Resistance Movement] Collective as well as the food vouchers that NUM [National Ugly Mugs] were providing. And [a former sex worker] friend [...] has gone onto Universal Credit after he was first furloughed [from a job outside sex work] then made redundant. He's talked about starting to escort again full-time. (Sebastian, male erotic masseur and independent escort)

In terms of the experience of participating in the original report, Fabian and Sebastian describe their experience as 'positive' or 'very positive' and Edmund hopes that such research would contribute to destigmatizing and making the industry safer. Fabian felt more outreach and education was needed, however, and this chimes with Beatrice's concern in Chapter 3 that, while a well-written or fair report is welcome, it needs also to be read widely and acted upon to have material impact.

Fenton's observation is a trenchant challenge to all academics and social researchers. He sees the interviews and consultations with unpaid participants about their lived and often difficult experiences as 'like a colonialist prospecting in other Nations for what can be sold' (Fenton, male independent escort, adult film actor and sexual health activist). While payment (beyond perhaps travel, childcare or a small voucher) is not allowed under research ethics as it is thought to compromise informed consent and free participation in research, it is true, as I observed in Chapter 1, that asking people to share their stories comes with some responsibility. This includes representing their experience and opinions faithfully (and not selectively) and keeping in mind that participant stories are real lives rather than currency for career or political agenda advancement.

Fenton also believes support for decriminalization will increasingly become a requirement from some organizations asked by researchers to act as gatekeepers in accessing participants. Organizations have a duty to protect their members or service-users from harm and have always assessed carefully, and sometimes declined requests by researchers to distribute invitations to participate in research. Fenton takes this a step further in requiring not just a commitment to ethical, critical and fair research but also to a particular legal model. One view would be that social research is always political and social science academics are not uncommonly engaged also in activism either outside of, or through, their work. This is because their work is both a job and a vocation and they want to use their privilege and access to knowledge to help to make change. Academic activism is, however, not unproblematic. De Castro Leal et al (2021, p 14) use the concept 'community fetishism' to describe 'the possible exploitation of communities that are constructed to be in need of help through activist-leaning research'. Harm can occur not just when so-called 'vulnerable groups' are fetishized but also when groups have their stories voiced through academics – a central tension in this book (see Chapter 2). A further risk of academic activism is that academics join a campaign echo chamber and blunt their key tool: critique, looking out *but also within*. These tensions are not resolved easily but are core to research on the sex industry, and other areas of social life.

Conclusion

Male independent sex workers are a significant minority within the UK sex industry. In the main, they see male clients, though a small number see couples and female clients. Work tends to be facilitated online through adult service websites, social media or personal websites. Male workers appear to be more likely than female workers to work independently, although some will work with others from a premises or do duo bookings. Morris (2018) describes 'incidental' encounters of 'casual, occasional, unsolicited commercial sex' between gay, bisexual and queer men and consultations during the Home Office data collection period similarly recognized forms of unplanned paid sex on the gay street scene, which would not necessarily be identified by those involved as 'sex work' (Hester et al, 2019, p 11). Some male-to-male sex work practices can be interpreted in the context of, but should not be conflated with, the historic persecution of gay or gender nonconforming men.

The participants in this chapter acknowledged their privilege as White males, but also their vulnerabilities as carers, as migrants or negotiating financial precarity, for example. They mentioned the burden of stigma and working often in secrecy but also their engagement in activism related to sex work and sexual health, including around PrEP and HIV, and commitment to volunteering in the wider community. Like female sex workers, the participants in the study all advocated for decriminalization; for access to online marketing platforms; and, more prominently within this group, law reform around censorship in the production of adult content.

5

Managed Brothel Workers

In law in England and Wales, there is no statutory definition of a 'brothel'. In *Winter v Woolfe* (1931), it was held to be 'a place where people of opposite sexes are allowed to resort for illicit intercourse, whether ... common prostitutes or not'. Section 6 of the Sexual Offences Act 1967 extended the definition to include same-sex relations. *Gorman v Standen, Palace Clarke v Standen* (1964) established that '[a] house occupied by one woman and used by her alone for prostitution, is not a brothel' and *Stevens v Christy* (1987) found that a brothel constitutes two or more individuals present or working in rotation. Premises where individual rooms or flats are let out to individuals offering sexual services may be classed as a brothel if it can be shown that these individuals are effectively working together: this is the grey area occupied by massage parlours which operate openly in most towns and cities in England and Wales. The relevant offences in relation to brothels and brothel-keeping are contained in Sections 33–35 of the Sexual Offences Act 1956 and the Crown Prosecution Service (CPS) advises prosecutors to focus on charging those profiting or exploiting the vulnerability of others. Similarly, the charging of 'maids' – individuals who assist in the running of a brothel, from cleaning to reception work – should, according to CPS guidance, be proportionate and in the public interest.

Research and media statements over recent years by the English Collective of Prostitutes (ECP) and the Sex Work Advocacy and Resistance Movement (SWARM) suggest however that brothel law enforcement has been used disproportionately against migrant women, for detention and deportation, rather than to safeguard (see, for example, SWARM's shadow report for CEDAW, 2019). In addition, some sex workers are working together for safety (in *cooperative brothels*) as we have seen in Chapters 3 and 4, where perhaps one sex worker owns or rents the premises, whereas others may work in *managed brothels*, run and/or owned by a third party (see Pitcher, 2015, for discussion on these different models). Managed brothels, which include massage parlours, some private flats or saunas, will often have a receptionist, security measures and charge sex workers commission and fees. It is this latter group that is the focus of this chapter.

Participant narratives (original email interview)

In this section are presented longer narratives from Titania (female independent escort and brothel worker) and Emilia (female former brothel worker). The excerpts are followed by discussion, drawing in also brief quotes from experiences from other participants who gave first interviews in the original research.

Titania's story (female independent escort and brothel worker)

I first traded money for sex in October 2016 after being propositioned by men on a dating site. I began working formally in January 2017 after roughly a month of unemployment and previous bad experiences in my degree field (exploitation at work, poor mental health) by placing an outcall only ad on [an adult service website]. Within three days I was able to pay off my outstanding rent and bills. Although I had intended it to be a stopgap, I found that I was able to meet my needs both financially and in terms of having enough time to look after my mental health, as well as enjoying the work, so I continued and transitioned into a combination of independent out-calls and brothel work.

I have been working intermittently for two years. Sex work is my sole income and occupation, but I have taken several breaks to go travelling. This has been funded by my sex work. I am not currently studying but am enrolled in a study abroad programme next year and hope to apply for a Masters degree in 2019.

For my independent work, I organise my own appointments either via phone or email (mostly email as I no longer publish my phone number). I have my own website and advertising which I have sole control over. For my brothel work, I am advertised by them on their website and Twitter using photos and a service list that I provide, although I do have the option of using the in-house photographer. The clients contact the brothel directly on the days that I'm working and book appointments, or in some locations they operate on a walk-in basis. I got my first brothel job by filling out the online recruitment form available on their website, but for other places I had to look for their number and phone the receptionist, leave my details and wait for a call-back. There was often a wait of several days for a shift, or some kind of trial period.

For my independent work, there is no-one else involved in the entire process. For my brothel work, the receptionist takes the bookings for me, and then when I'm in the room with the client they give me the money, which I keep in my bag. At the end of each shift, the receptionist counts up my appointments and I pay a portion of my earnings to the house.

I prefer to work in a brothel environment. I have tried independent work in hotels, but I generally feel very unsafe when doing this as I have previously received threats from people who are aware that I am working alone, and I do not feel able to get help from the on-site security. In a brothel I feel safer as there are other people around, the management employ security, and there is a receptionist to deal with difficult clients if I want them to leave. As an independent worker I would have to deal with them myself, which risks them becoming violent, but in a brothel, I am able to leave the room whilst the receptionist (or security if it is a serious issue) escorts them out. Another reason I choose to work in brothels is that it means I am able to provide in-calls (which account for the vast majority of the market) without taking on any financial risks, such as renting a hotel room or flat, hiring my own security, or paying an assistant to handle enquiries, as I am not in a position where I can afford to lose significant amounts of money.

There is as vast a range of sex worker experiences, just as there are client experiences. I find it interesting that the question about clients' motivations came much higher up the list [of email interview questions], as clients' feelings are not really relevant to the discussion of sex work. Out of my work friends, I know that many are single mothers, some are students, and I have met a few career sex workers who are either happy in the job, also work in other areas of the industry (such as porn) or just don't know what else to do (either no skills in other sectors or no particular desire to do anything else). Many of my friends are migrant sex workers from eastern Europe who intend to work for a few years in order to set themselves up in their home country.

[The benefits of sex work are that] I have complete financial and personal freedom. I am able to pay all my bills and live comfortably, whilst having enough time to take care of my mental health. I have a flexible, well-paying job.

[In terms of the challenges and risks, I would identify] the stigma perpetuated by politicians and the media. Because of the constant negative dialogue around sex work, I feel I have to hide my occupation from my family and wider friend group. I believe that the 'feminist' dialogue of sex work as violence against women sends the message that we deserve to experience violence. I also sometimes worry that my sex work history may affect me if I wish to transition into other work in the future.

As a sex worker I am always at a risk of violence, primarily because of the stigma as discussed in the previous paragraph. I take as many precautions as possible, such as screening clients, having a safe call and only taking in-calls at brothels. I have, however, never had a violent encounter in my two years of working.

The main harm I experience is the mental trauma of privileged women trying to use my life to score political goals. Having my experiences constantly talked over and disregarded so that they can push a narrative that actively contributes to the risks to my personal safety is dehumanising, and their attempts to legislate my community out of existence is the most degrading thing I have ever experienced.

There are fewer clients now than ever before. Business has slowed for everybody, and I have heard anecdotally from friends I work with that it is the worst it has ever been. At the same time, there are more people engaging in sex work, I believe due to the extreme austerity measures imposed by the Conservative government. This means that that the market is much more competitive. We are having to work a lot more often, the work is less flexible, we are less able to turn down clients and many women are now offering more services for lower prices than they would have done previously.

Emilia's story (female former brothel worker)

I got started at the age of fifteen. I was in [name of country] and had recently been kicked out of home by my conservative Christian parents for being gay. A few girls I ended up meeting worked for this lady called Karen who ran a brothel and a strip club, and the girls lived with her. Karen sent the girls to invite me up to the brothel to have a drink and a chat, which I did, and she was only too happy to give me a room in her house and to have me start work the next night. From that point on I lived with Karen, and it was not too bad – she cooked and cleaned for us. We were like a family, and I enjoyed it very much. We were able to use her car and live in her house and it was a nice house. Then I came to England at age 20 and started working in the brothels in [name of town] because it was the only thing I knew how to do or where to turn. I moved to England to live with [a family member] who is wonderful and also cooked and cleaned and gave me a home, but I did not know how to live in England anymore (I had originally moved to [name of country] as a ten year old). I did not know how to find work, how to use public transport, banking or even where to go to buy a pair of trousers. It was very difficult. So, I went online and found the [brothel directory], which pointed me in the direction of brothels nearby. I rang one of them up and started work there the following night. For the purposes of this research, I will write about my time working in England only.

I worked full-time, meaning 60 hours plus. Some shifts were 24-hour shifts. I ended up working at a number of different brothels all round [city in England], usually at the same time as most places only wanted you to work a night or two a week so the customers didn't get bored of seeing you. You usually had a set night – for example Wednesday and that was your night you were put online and advertised as being available and [the brothel management] could take advanced bookings for you. In the nicer places they would charge £50 for half an hour; the not so nice was £40 and they would usually do a 15-minute type deal for £30 at the cheaper places. The customer would come in and pay the receptionist who took the booking, and we would get £30, £25 and £20 respectively.

For an hour it was generally £60 we would get, no matter where you worked – but they were allowed to have sex twice for that. Every parlour takes all the money for your first booking though, to pay the receptionist. [So] basically you do the first job free, then every tenth job you owe the receptionist £10 and fifteenth £20 then you have to pay the doorman £10 or £20 depending.

Because of the area I worked, 80 percent of the clients were Pakistani or other Asian origin. Ten percent were young White men usually drunk or high, and 5 percent were old White men; the other five percent were [an]other [ethnicity]. As for their motivations, I usually worked nights so I would say being on cocaine was the driving factor for 90 percent: the old White guys were just having affairs. I worked usually with 3 or four other girls on shift. I enjoyed this. We were all friendly and we would chat and drink and do cocaine together and have fun.

I would say that most of the girls I worked with were English, but about 30 percent of them were from Eastern Europe and their motivations were purely monetary, I would say. They never drank, they never did drugs, they never bought takeaways, they never had fun or joined in our laughs: they were very work focussed. The rest of us seemed to have no homes to go to, or friends, and [had experienced] a breakdown in family relationships – so it was very much a replacement family to most of us, it seemed.

The benefits to myself, as I have touched upon, were friendship, family and a way of life – as well as earning money. I do not feel I benefitted anybody else (except line the owners' pockets), nor would I have wanted to.

Challenges included having to take a booking when you really did not want to, when you were tired or coming off drugs or the customer was really drunk and difficult: that is a challenge. [In terms of risks], well, anybody could do anything to you really, especially when you were in the upstairs rooms, and nobody could hear you scream. Looking back, I can see how it was harmful, with the drug culture and the way we were treated and used – but at the time I did not see this.

I have not seen any changes myself, but the older workers used to talk about the good old days when there was more money: the clients had more money, the owners used to pay more, and everything sounded generally better.

I am now married to a wonderful woman who took me out of that world, I had a child (to a customer who has no idea) and I work in [social care] which I love, so my future plans are to keep doing what I am doing hopefully.

I do not believe that the sex industry should be legalised. [In England] I have watched brothels be shut down and the owners marched off with my own eyes and I have enjoyed every minute of seeing their assets seized and having to go to court. It makes me happy because of all the times we had money held over our heads (our money that we had earned that night, we did not get it given to us until the end of the night, it could be essentially taken from us at any time); to have to see drunk, violent men when we were exhausted or being forced to do things we did not want to do and just being told to get back in the room and deal with it. I was tired of having sex with three or four men and ending up with ten pounds after paying the receptionist and doorman and transport there. I was glad there was some justice: there is nothing but evil in them. They will not lie on their own backs but have everybody else do it for them at any cost and I am glad that it is illegal to make profit from somebody else's body in this country!

Discussion of first interviews

In this section, I discuss both the narratives presented in the previous section and draw on the wider first interview data. This analysis is set out in five parts, as explained in Chapter 2, namely: routes in; benefits; harms; hoped-for changes in the industry; and future plans.

Titania's entry into sex work was initially a stopgap but has become her main occupation: it pays well, enables her to manage better her mental wellbeing and to afford periods of travel. She noted her experience of work exploitation *prior* to entering the sex industry but speaks positively of managed brothels, where client bookings and premises are organized for her, and security provided. Emilia's entry was somewhat different. Her conservative parents did not accept her coming out as gay and she was encouraged through contacts into the care of Karen, who ran a brothel and strip club. Later moving back to the UK, Emilia found it hard to reintegrate into English life and sought out local brothels for work. She enjoyed the camaraderie of working with other girls and being able to chat and laugh between bookings. However, Emilia is scathing about management practices, in particular the high commissions and extra fees charged. The 2019 Home Office report (Hester et al, 2019) highlighted other practices such as withholding payment or profiting unofficially from 'extras', including unprotected sex:

> In the brothel, my manager charges them money to come into the building then agrees a price with them. I take the money from the room to the lounge so they can check it for fakes, and in the room, I discuss extras with clients (things like oral without a condom). The managers don't want to hear about extras because there's a proper shop front and they have their line about 'whatever happens in the room is between the two of you' so I keep the money, but they don't let you charge more than £20 for extras and always say that they find out from clients how much you charge extra and stuff. Reception takes their cut (around 50%) and then any fees – we have 'facilities fees' where they charge us for stuff like bedding and locker use – and then give us the money when we're done. I'm not allowed to tell clients how much money I'm getting. If we don't get any clients, we still have to pay facilities fees, so sometimes they send us to the cash point to pay them (female brothel worker). (Hester et al, 2019, p 17)

Commonly in discussions about exploitation in the sex industry, the concern is about exploitation of vulnerability, sexual violence, consent and coercion, and gender inequality. In these accounts (see similarly for erotic dancers in Chapter 6), some participants identify working conditions in managed premises as a key harm. These issues can be interrelated: Emilia describes in her second interview how, in her experience, more ruthless brothel operators would not support women in declining known violent clients or come to their aid when they called for help from the room. Since parlours operate in a legal twilight, financial and operating data is not published, workers are rarely unionized, vacancies can be easily backfilled and some workers may be constrained to move by money, transport, childcare or other reasons: management hold much of the power. The Health and Safety Executive inspects only legal premises; sex establishments are regulated by local councils under Sexual Entertainment Venue (SEV) legislation (provisions in the Policing and Crime Act 2009 amended Schedule 3 of the Local Government [Miscellaneous Provisions Act 1982]) and do not include brothels; brothels fall under the ambit of the local police force. And so, unless they come to the attention of law enforcement, the labour practices of managed brothels are under-scrutinized, often to the detriment of sex workers. In her email feedback on this chapter, Titania noted that 'the likely outcome of reporting a brothel is that the entire business is shut down and the worker in question gets blacklisted by other owners, as well as putting their colleagues out of a job'.

Titania also raises the issue of stigma and the heated media debates on the sex industry, in particular 'privileged women trying to use my life to score political goals'. Her observation reminds us of the material impact of discourse. Whether on social media or in public conversation, we can become so gripped by social issues in abstract and often selective terms that we may lose sight of the personhood of those discussed. It is true that policy at the macro level cannot meet each conflicting need: Titania and Emilia's views of brothel work are different, for example. But they do share common ground that working with others feels safer and provides the opportunity to offload emotionally.

Participant reflections (second email interview)

Second interviews with Titania and Emilia were conducted in spring 2021.

Titania's reflection (female independent escort and brothel worker)

I have now exited the sex industry and no longer live in the UK, and so I am reflecting on my interview with significant distance. However, I still feel that the answers I gave then are broadly aligned with my current feelings around the industry. Since leaving sex work I have spent a lot of time processing my experiences and I still feel that the main harms I experienced were rooted in the political narrative around sex work rather than the work itself. Overall, I feel positive about my time in the industry and vastly prefer it to my current job both in terms of earning potential and flexibility. If I were to return to the UK, I would strongly consider re-entering the sex industry.

Since I have left the industry, I don't have first-hand experience of the impact of COVID-19, however I can imagine that the effect has been devastating. Due to the unstable nature of the business, an unexpected gap in earnings is likely to hit many workers very hard. I am currently living in [name of country], so my life has been almost completely unaffected by COVID, and I am very glad that I was not in the UK during this time. Although I was earning a comfortable amount as a sex worker, I do think I would have seriously struggled to support myself over the past year and may have taken on more dangerous work to survive. However, this is not an issue unique to sex work as this is the nature of all freelance employment, and many of my friends who are self-employed have also had difficulty supporting themselves and have either had to find other work or rely on support from family members.

I do believe that the report represented my experiences, as well as a range of other experiences that do not align with my own. My main criticism of the report was the inclusion of client voices. As mentioned in my previous follow-up interview, client voices are entirely irrelevant to the 'debate' around sex work, as it is rather like asking somebody who eats hamburgers what they think about the McDonalds' strike. I am aware that the APPG[1] who commissioned the research had a particular outcome (that all sex work is exploitative and should be eradicated) they wanted when they did so, and this is the case for most discussion around sex work, as sex workers are rarely (if ever) listened to or centred in the discussion.

I hope that future research can be conducted without focusing on client motivations and just centre the voices of actual sex workers who are affected by the policies informed by this research. As a now former sex worker, I do not feel able to publicly defend the sex work community using my own experiences as this would very likely cause me to lose my current job and residency status, so more anonymised research of this nature is very valuable in defending the community which I still strongly identify with.

Emilia's reflection (female former brothel worker)

I stand by everything I wrote in my original email interview. In fact, I am even more determined that sex work should not be legalised in the sense that it allows brothel owners to operate with impunity [but I believe in] the decriminalisation of the sex workers themselves.

My daughter (by marriage) has just turned [late teens] and I look at her and her friends and realise just how young I was and how I was very much taken advantage of.

I mean even in how the money for the first job was immediately taken from you to pay the receptionist; then half of the second job. And after, say, five customers you had to give [the management] a tenner; then after ten [customers], you had to pay [the management] an extra £20 on top. Then £20 for the security and they have already taken half of the money that the customer pays to begin with!

And a few places I worked would pay you at the end and keep the money in a time locked safe. That meant you could not refuse a customer or leave the shift because the safe didn't open until 9 o'clock: so, you wouldn't get paid, basically.

And the rule of thumb was, if you missed a shift for whatever reason, you lost two extra shifts without exception. That leaves you screwed then, basically, as lots of girls don't even have ID or bank accounts to get benefits or anything to fall back on. I worked with one girl who came to work with tuberculosis for months. When I was a teenager, I had an abortion in the morning and came to work that very same night.

Looking at that now I'm 30, and seeing these young girls, my heart would absolutely break for them. And obviously I would wish that the clients would get prosecuted: I loathe and detest the vast majority of them. It knocks me sick, the very idea.

Many a time I've known girls to be locked in the room with customers who are drunk and violent. Once I was attacked in a bathroom at a [named] hotel and wasn't able to leave until I gave the customer his money back. And let me tell you, you soon learn that [name of hotel chain] bathrooms are soundproof. When I eventually managed to escape, I ran to the hotel front desk to ask them to call the police: they took one look at me and wanted me off the premises. To add insult to injury, the same man a week later came into [the brothel] where I worked and booked me for an hour! I told the receptionist what had gone on and she said, 'Well, he's a regular,' and that was that.

I've had awful interactions with the police. Once I reported a rape and literally got told by the investigating police officer, 'Well, I don't know why you're reporting this: you're a prostitute. Why does it matter? What's one more man?' I even had a baby with a customer who pulled the condom off. I went through with the pregnancy because I was desperate to be out of the sex industry. I met my amazing wife and now have a wonderful life [with my child too], which I never thought possible. So yes, I definitely appreciate being part of this whole study if there's even a sliver of a chance of it being used to help anybody at all. Nobody has ever before asked me any of this and a lot of times I've been desperate to tell my story. However, we are not deemed worthy to listen to, it seems.

Discussion of second interviews

By the time of the second interviews, Titania, like Emilia, had left the sex industry. She feels lucky to have left the UK and secured new employment just before COVID-19 hit. She maintains that the principal harms that she experienced in sex work were stigma and judgement – and says she would consider re-entering if she came back to the UK. Titania expresses a tension in wanting to speak out for sex workers; yet at the same time, she is conscious that she has now left and that identifying publicly may inhibit her career progression. There has been research looking at becoming an ex-sex worker in terms of the personal and structural factors which facilitate change (notably Sanders, 2007), on managing sex worker identities (for example, Ma et al, 2018), on post-exit trauma and identity recovery for those who have experienced commercial sexual exploitation (for example, Hom and Woods, 2013), and on how sex workers become activist and work with external allies (for example, Chowdhury, 2006; Smith and Mac, 2020). However, there is less work on how *former* sex workers manage an identity and a community which has been an important part of their life, and whom they want to campaign for, but that they fear would undermine their present and future.

On the theme of re-opening the past, Emilia's sense of release both in documenting, and making sense of, what happened to her is palpable.

> Nobody has ever before asked me any of this and a lot of times I've been desperate to tell my story. However, we are not deemed worthy to listen to, it seems. (Emilia, female former brothel worker)

Having her child and meeting her partner have been life changing. As Emilia reflects on her experiences, she feels firmly that the managed brothel model does not work and serves only to line the pockets of those whom, as she described in her first interview, would not themselves 'lie on [their] backs'. Titiania's experience, and therefore her assessment, of the managed brothel is different. In email feedback on this chapter, she says:

> I have never worked later than 8pm [and] any worker caught drinking alcohol or taking drugs on premises or offering unprotected PIV [penis-in-vagina] sex would be fired immediately in 5 out of 7 places I have worked (at least, the other two I cannot confirm either way).

She notes too that the brothel with the highest fees that she paid was 'the only place I have worked that is run by a former sex worker'. Titania is keen to emphasize that she had a certain amount of privilege, in the sense that she had options through education, stable citizenship, housing and no dependents, for example. On balance, she believes the personal context of the workers and the legal status of managed brothels informs the experience of working in this setting.

The difference in opinion and experience between the participants reminds us that sex workers are not a homogenous group. Some will feel bound nevertheless by a collective identity and understanding of what it is to work in the sex industry. Drawing on Bakhtin (2004 [1986]) and Tracy (2010), I noted in Chapter 2 the benefit of reflecting on and re-visiting the research process with participants and visibilizing those contestations to the reader. It is not always possible given timeframes and respect for participants' unpaid time. But where it can be done, it forces some transparency into the process of academic and policy report-writing, including reflection on how and whose evidence is selected to justify the conclusions reached.

Conclusion

This chapter considered the experience of sex workers in managed brothels, where a third party provides the premises, a receptionist and often security and cleaning facilities. Titania and Emilia had divergent views on this model of labour – because they had different experiences of it – although both noted the value of being with others for safety and companionship, when needed. The narratives and excerpts here suggest that managed brothels operate outside of labour regulatory regimes (such as health and safety or licensing) and so the potential for work exploitation is significant. This means that while the physical risks faced by sex workers are always there, the work conditions may exacerbate (or ameliorate) these.

In the second interviews, Titania had left sex work, but unlike Emilia, who had moved career and started a family and was strongly critical of the brothel industry, Titania felt that it had given her flexibility and financial freedom, and she would return if needed. Both women expressed that anonymity was important in terms of protecting their present and future, although in email correspondence Emilia said that increasingly she would be prepared to speak on the record if needed. Titania described the tension of leaving an identity and community which she still felt strongly about. Both experiences reflect the long shadow of stigma and managing the past.

6

Erotic Dancers and Strippers

Erotic dance, exotic dance, stripping and striptease are all forms of performance designed to aesthetically and sexually stimulate the viewer. Some settings will maintain a clear boundary between dancers and clientele, enforcing a 'no-contact' rule; in other contexts, dance may be combined (officially or unofficially) with direct contact activity. In England and Wales, 'any premises at which relevant entertainment [for example: lap dancing, table dancing, pole dancing or strip shows] is provided before a live audience for the financial gain of the organiser or the entertainer' constitutes a Sexual Entertainment Venue (SEV) and is defined in law under section 27 of the Policing and Crime Act 2009. Local councils are charged with assessing and granting a license to operate SEVs.

Research in England has looked at the emergence, impact and resistance to the revised SEV licensing rules (see Hubbard, 2009; Hubbard and Colosi, 2015). Katy Pilcher's (2012a, 2012b, 2017) work explores female spectatorship of both female and male dancers. The dancers whose stories are presented here performed in strip pubs and clubs predominantly for male customers, although women may also have been part of the audience. As the narratives in this chapter show, Sanders and Hardy's insight in 2012 (p 53) that 'the industry has maintained its market presence due to its ability to establish highly financially exploitative employment relationships with dancers at a time of economic fragility' appears to hold true. While the public and political discourse about SEVs has tended to focus on gender equality and community impact, groups such as the East London Strippers Collective and United Sex Workers campaign in the UK for labour rights, safety and transparent management within strip venues.

Participant narratives (original email interview)

In this section are presented longer narratives from Imogen (a stripper) and Isabella (an independent escort, stripper and sugar baby). The excerpts are followed by discussion, drawing in also brief quotes from experiences from other participants who gave first interviews in the original research.

Imogen's story (female stripper)

I started through a series of auditions – it took me a long time to get hired. For several years I worked 4–5 days a week: sometimes doing double shifts on the same day. It was a full-time job during those years and then I went down to three shifts a week. I am now down to a handful of shifts a month.

Shifts were booked either directly with the house mum (dancer supervisor) at the venue or via an agent. The venue websites would advertise my name on their listings/calendar page. I communicate with my regulars directly to tell them when I am in a venue local to them. I was not recruited. I actively went in search of stripping as a career – yes, despite having been a professional and having a degree I actively chose to be a stripper.

[Payment] depends on the venue: some venues take their house fee, and all other takings are the dancers' to keep. Other venues take a house fee and then you have to pay commission on your dances at the end of the shift. Other venues require all payments to go through the manager first and then they pay you out at the end of the night. Separate to that is the fee I paid to my booking agent.

[Clients are] very varied. Often heterosexual male but other than that they were/are of all ages, races, income brackets, religions and motivations. Some were there just for a bit of fun, to add some randomness to their routines, others come in to fill a gap in their intimate life – perhaps their wife isn't affectionate or sexual with them, or they don't have a partner.

[Have you been involved in other areas of the sex industry?] I've tried a bit of domination but, other than that, no.

In the venues I have mainly worked at (strip pubs which have a smaller number of girls), girls tend to work together quite well if a group of customers present themselves. Sometimes this would be challenging: we all have different levels of contact and modes of working that we are comfortable with. For the most part though, working in groups wasn't a problem and can be welcome if you aren't quite on your game that night. Sometimes I do better when one-on-one with a customer as I can better use my rapport-building skills.

Strippers are often women with some options – contrary to some external narratives. My observation would be that in general, they don't tend to be on the breadline, though they might have financial problems here and there like anyone else in any other sector. Stripping is a sales job based on 100% commission: the psychology of this makes it hard to pull off for most people who are really hard up. I had a professional career before I started dancing: most girls start in their early 20s. I meet girls who don't have the same background/education as me, but I have only ever met one dancer who was clearly genuinely destitute (living out of plastic bags and sofa-surfing).

[Benefits include that] I made more money than I had in a while, which was amazing (though I don't think strippers earn as much as they used to − I would probably have earned more had I stayed in my previous profession, and with less anxiety around unsteady income). [...] I have become very good at dealing with difficult people. [...] I loved dancing on stage − this was my original motivator to start, along with needing to make some cash. [...] I have faced and overcome some deep-seated insecurities. [...] I got my yen for performing out of my system − I had been on course to be a performer as a teenager but came off the rails and regretted that. [...] I know that [I have] helped people through difficult periods of depression.

Those strippers who survive the course and make money have very strong mindsets. It is hard never knowing how much you are going to make (though strip pubs offer more financial consistency than strip clubs). At first it is hard to overcome the constant rejection, but you get used to this, particularly once you tap into the stripper training there is online.

It is also difficult, in an environment where alcohol is flowing freely, to police your own personal boundaries, particularly if you are in an unlicensed venue where the no-touching rule is not enforced. But this depends on the dancer: just like people in any walk of life, there are some who are great at personal boundaries and others who are not.

The negative side of [stripping] is having to keep the whole job under wraps. Being in the closet has had very negative impacts on my life and finding [a collective] made that easier to deal with. I would like to be able to talk about my work experiences from stripping now I am moving into a new career as I have developed some major skills and achievements there, but instead I am frightened that I will get outed, and it will skewer my new career path.

Another negative [...] is being tied into anti-social hours − my agent, who often misused the power that came with that position, would require us to book shifts 6 weeks or more in advance, and this meant that, as a single woman with a mortgage to support, I was on a treadmill of being cut off from my friends and wider society because of the hours.

The biggest negative impact of this job is the manipulation and disregard from some managers and owners. It makes my blood boil that local councils fixate on whether there is touching going on, when they never look at basic health and safety in the premises or whether the management is randomly changing fees, or charging women for being ill, or firing them at the drop of a hat (all of which has happened to me). The stigma attached to stripping, the way that dancers can be dropped from a club without warning, and its freedoms in terms of mobility and shift patterns, mean that till now girls have not tended to challenge this, or even openly talk about it in public.

Another risk I see, which hasn't affected me, but I see in other, younger, women, is the potential to develop disdain for male sexuality. This is a natural risk in any job where people have the same pattern of interaction repeatedly with others: academics complain about students, retail assistants complain about customers, taxi drivers complain about passengers, etc. It is that easy-to-do othering and complaining that is also so accepted in British culture. However, in this kind of job, that disdain could impact subsequent personal relationships. I said to myself I would stop as soon as I started to hate men for their sexuality and that has never happened, because I am committed to sex positivity and compassion. Nevertheless, I [do] find myself making the sweeping generalisation [of feeling antipathy towards certain clients].

Another risk is that you can become desensitised to sexuality and your own erogenous zones. This is no different to the natural acclimatisation that happens in many jobs, but it does impact your own intimate relationships.

And finally, there is the deleterious impact upon body image of being semi-naked in front of mirrors all day long as well as working in a rarefied environment (because the anti-social hours and social stigma can cut you off from wider society) where plastic surgery and cosmetology are so widespread. You would be surprised how many venues have terrible overhead fluorescent lighting in the (sometimes inadequate and sometimes unsafe) changing rooms which show every horrible crease and crack in your skin that isn't visible under normal light.

I work just 6 times a month now. I have a new business venture I am working on. I want to keep helping the drive to unionise [strippers]. I have had some ★terrible★ experiences at the hands of management. […] I have considered ways of getting revenge but think that channelling that anger and sense of injustice into the unionising drive is the most positive use of my energy.

The best thing the government can do is to accept that sexual entertainment will never go away. It would be amazing if the authorities wised up to what was really happening in strip clubs and helped the industry modernise. Why do they listen to misinformed and blind feminists who have never been inside a venue (and don't know how deeply human the interaction between stripper and customer can be), over and above those people who are in these venues day in, day out?

Why are they hell-bent in closing down venues when the transactions happening inside are between consensual adults, and often have a therapeutic or mental health benefit for the customer? Much worse things are happening elsewhere in the UK (and the human race is facing extinction through climate change). If this isn't for religious and moral reasons, then what is it for?

Isabella's story (female independent escort, stripper, sugar baby)

I started stripping 3 years ago when I had just turned 19, as a way of funding a gap year to travel. It was something I had always wanted to do so I went to my local club to audition.

In the first year of working, I only did stripping and did 3/4 nights a week. Now I am studying full-time too, so I work 2 days a week as an escort in addition to 'strippergram' work for stag parties etc. whenever they come up which is usually a couple of times a month [and work in strip clubs in the holidays].

For most clubs you just email/phone them or turn up on the day and audition and they say yes or no. All clubs have different expectations regarding days worked etc. With the agency I work with for strippergram jobs, I just emailed them some pictures and then they started sending me jobs.

With most clubs you have to pay a 'house fee' at the beginning of your shift which can range from £10 to in the hundreds, often in addition to a % commission at the end of the night, which may vary depending on how many dances you've done or how busy the club was that night. At the end of the night, you cash out and receive your money cash in hand, although some clubs work differently and pay you periodically e.g., once a week. This way can be difficult because they sometimes try and underpay you. Also, when a customer pays for a dance or VIP time with a card, you usually receive chips or vouchers that you cash in with the club at the end of your shift. Often when you get a card transaction, the club takes a higher percentage of that transaction than they would with cash. With agency work, they take commission, although the amount varies depending on the job and often the clients pay that directly to them in advance, and I receive my fee in cash when I arrive at the job. Other times I receive the full amount and bank transfer the commission over to the agency.

There's a huge variety among [clients] from young to old etc. However, I have found that (particularly in escorting) the clients who spend the most money or are regulars are often middle-aged and just looking for female company above anything else. In strip clubs, it's often the same, except there are the younger stag parties and businessmen taking their clients out.

Out of all the different types of sex work I've done [stripping, escorting, webcamming, sugar dating] I find stripping/lapdancing to be my favourite as I feel clubs are the safest of these workplaces, as well as the fact that I love performing and the stage work.

I think everyone in sex work has different motivations and experiences in the industry because it's such a personal thing and everyone varies in their attitudes and approaches to the work that they undertake. I have many friends working across all areas of the industry, and they vary in demographics, but I would say that most people's motivations for entering the industry are purely financial and because it offers a far more flexible way of living than other industries, especially for students who can't commit to a fixed amount of hours. In terms of experience, I've been lucky so far not to have experienced anything awful, but I have friends who unfortunately can't say the same.

Benefits for me include flexible working hours, the ability to work almost anywhere in the world, the opportunity to earn far more than in other jobs and also being exposed to so many different situations/people/places which has given me invaluable life experience. For the most part I really enjoy my job and I think my work benefits my clients in varying ways, from simply providing fun and entertainment to being almost like a friend and someone to connect with.

I think all kinds of sex work carry unique emotional challenges for workers and it can be very harmful for your mental health if you don't have adequate support from friends, other workers and organisations. Social stigma surrounding the industry also contributes to harm caused to workers because they often feel unable to seek help or even discuss the nature of their work with others.

It's also really hard to organise jobs as there aren't many places to actually work safely (for escorting but also stripping because councils seem increasingly focussed on closing down our clubs), or even discuss it with other workers online as the internet and social media platforms are becoming increasingly censored and keep blocking our accounts. This is detrimental to our community because it takes away our support network and pushes everything further underground. Under SESTA/FOSTA [Fight Online Sex Trafficking Act/Stop Enabling Sex Traffickers Act] in the United States, some websites have even been taken down that would have provided workers with information about dangerous clients. The effects of this can clearly been seen as [violent] incident rates have gone up dramatically.

I have only been in the industry for 3 years so I can't comment too much on changes over time although I have seen online censorship increase, and the number of strip venues decrease whilst their house fees and commission rates increase despite the number of customers and the amount of money they spend decrease.

I don't have any fixed plans at the moment, but I graduate this year (2019) and I'd like to find a good job related to my course [in the UK or Europe]. I think I will stay in sex work for the foreseeable future as I enjoy it and it provides me the opportunity to live the lifestyle I want.

Discussion of first interviews

In this section, I discuss both the narratives presented in the previous section and draw on the wider first interview data. This analysis is set out in five parts, as explained in Chapter 2, namely: routes in; benefits; harms; hoped-for changes in the industry; and future plans.

Both participants were clear that they actively chose to start stripping and described it as a performance art as well as a way of earning money. Imogen saw herself as unusual in entering stripping after working professionally outside the sex industry: she auditioned a number of times and persisted until she was successful. Isabella similarly loved the 'performing and the stage work' as well as feeling safer, relatively, than when escorting. Both participants identified the potential for earning a significant amount of money and flexibly as a key benefit. Imogen recognized the people skills that she had developed yet would not be able to evidence in her CV, given the stigma around stripping. Isabella similarly felt that the job had given her an early and extraordinary insight into people and places.

Challenges articulated by Imogen and Isabella included the risk of developing an unhealthy body image, of dissociating from one's own sensuality or from men in general, and of maintaining emotional wellbeing, which was made harder by the stigma and secrecy around their work. The management and pay for workers within strip venues were described as problematic and this chimed with responses from other dancers to the Home Office survey and follow-up interviews. For example:

In terms of risks, to my personal safety very minimal – I was always working indoors with colleagues. [...] I would have to pay the club a 'house fee' at the start of my shift and/or a percentage of commission from everything I earn in tips and lapdances. Many clubs increase these fees without any restrictions or consultation with dancers. [...] The main risk was just about losing money (if I paid a high house fee and then didn't make any money I would be out of pocket). [...] When stripclubs close, 'agencies' take their place. Anyone can operate an unregulated agency, booking strippers to perform at private events like stag parties, that often happen in flats or hotels, without the public accountability of an SEV, and where there are no limits on alcohol consumption or illegal drugs, and no safeguarding strategies in place. When strip clubs close, it makes sex workers even more invisible, and lulls the public into thinking the problem is solved. [...] In reality, patriarchy feeds off women's lack of choice. When women have fewer choices in the sex industry, less agency, less protection, fewer options – this hands power directly to the industry operators and consumers, who are overwhelmingly male. (Female stripper)

Poor enforcement of no-touching rules; the flow of alcohol; the minimal screening of clients as they enter the venue; competition between dancers for tips; and working often without a contract could make what one interviewee described as a 'toxic and unpleasant' atmosphere. Participants questioned the licensing preoccupation with sexual contact but the absence of regard for dancers' work and pay conditions. For this reason, Imogen wanted to see more dancers and strippers unionized to challenge management injustice in the sector.

As well as concerns about sexual contact within strip clubs, the public debate has also focused on whether SEVs contribute to, or reinforce, gender inequality (see, for example, the House of Commons Women and Equalities Committee 2018 hearing on Sexual Harassment of Women and Girls in Public). However, Imogen questioned why the already monitored existence of public strip clubs still garnered attention from policymakers given the abusive behaviour that continued, often unchallenged, in the private and domestic realm, or indeed through the 'non-SEV' night-time economy. For Isabella, an abolitionist approach – including online censorship and closure of clubs – only led to more violence and less choice for women. These arguments illustrate the contested nature of 'cause and effect' in debates on the sex industry: for some commentators, SEVs are both a reflection and a cause of gender inequality and violence against women; for others, participating in and consuming sexual entertainment is separate from, and does not constitute or condone, gendered violence.

Participant reflections (second email interview)

This section presents second interviews with Imogen and Isabella conducted in spring 2021.

Imogen's reflection (female stripper)

[Reading back through my original email interview], I stand by it, but I would soften and qualify some of the language. [...]

COVID-19 only served to highlight the inequalities faced by sex workers in this country. However, it's also enabled a greater sense of community as people have pivoted and supported each other and organised and some great things have come about as a result.

I don't think I saw the final [Home Office] report – I would be interested in doing so. I can't really remember much about [the original email interview] except writing my answers [in transit] as I had been super-busy.

[In terms of how sex workers are reflected in academic and government research broadly], I don't know because I haven't read enough of it. I do frequently see requests for comment come in from students though. It would be good if some academics were able to come out as having done sex work themselves because then there would be less of a gold-fish bowl feeling about being the subject of people's curiosity. However, I appreciate that's not possible. I think things will change.

Isabella's reflection (female independent escort, stripper, sugar baby)

[Reading back through my original email interview], it feels like a long time ago. I've now been in the industry 5 years and now escort independently with no agencies, which is a lot more admin for me but worth it, as I can keep all my money. I've also stopped sugaring because it was too much emotional labour for the pay off.

COVID-19 made the last year really hard. I was unable to work for much of the year as the clubs closed and escort clients disappeared, in addition to not being able to rent a hotel room to see them, leaving me with nowhere to work. At times I used friends' flats: however, this isn't ideal because it leaves me/my friends vulnerable to stalkers and bad clients. Myself and many other workers received no grants or financial support from the government so I was pushed to work online on [content subscription service], which I really do not enjoy.

The movement of many existing sex workers online, and also the influx of new workers who took up sex work online during the pandemic, meant competition was hugely increased and pushed prices even lower. Over the last month I returned to escorting work. However, there are still far fewer clients than usual, and I feel pressured to see clients I'm not 100% comfortable with because I have to make money somehow, and they are often the only option.

Increased censorship online has made advertising my online profile even more difficult as I can't post anything on Instagram without the threat of being deactivated. I was banned from Twitter for 'violating the media policy', even though I had no nudity or anything that was against their terms and conditions. This had a direct impact on my ability to earn, as I lost my platform, and felt especially unfair and targeted because I'm a sex worker advertising services, when countless other Twitter accounts freely post hardcore porn with no consequences.

Overall, the pandemic has further highlighted how inadequate policies are surrounding sex workers, as many of us have been left with no income, no support, no protection, increased vulnerabilities and not even a mention from the Government.

[In terms of the Home Office report], yes, I do feel my opinions and experiences were reflected accurately and I appreciated the chance to contribute to and [be able to] review the content [before its publication].

This is a step in the right direction as, for once, workers are speaking for themselves, not being spoken for/over. However, I still think much more needs to be done to push sex worker voices to the forefront of the conversation, and actually implement positive change regarding policy.

Discussion of second interviews

Isabella is now five years into sex working and, as her main source of income and work experience, the pandemic has been a real challenge. Strip venues have been closed and she has moved online and tried to venture back into escorting, this time independently to avoid agency fees. Like Fenton and Sebastian in Chapter 4, she has found online censorship problematic and erratically enforced. Imogen has started a new business venture but continues to be active around stripper wellbeing and conditions and the wider sex work community. Isabella was broadly happy with the final Home Office report and, while both Imogen and Isabella welcome work which facilitates sex worker voices directly, both feel this needs to be followed up with policy *action*.

Isabella is critical of the lack of government assistance during the pandemic and Imogen identifies that support has come primarily from within the sex work community. It is worth noting that some individuals who are not involved in direct 'full-service' sex work (including stripping, BDSM or webcamming, for example), may align or distance themselves from the term 'sex work' or 'sex worker' depending on self-perception, the service they provide and the degree of physical contact they have with clients. For example, Nayar (2017) observes that young women (and clients) engaged in sugar dating may not (want to) conceive this as 'sex work', even though the labour and rewards involved are materially similar to escorting. McNeill (2012) frames this in terms of a 'whorearchy', where roles within the sex industry are differentiated and implicitly privileged. Individuals should be free to identify themselves as they wish and, from the wider Home Office survey data, it was clear that for some the label of 'sex worker' was simply a term that made sense for explaining how they earn money. However, for others, including Isabella and Imogen, 'sex worker' is to varying degrees a political identity: an indicator of solidarity with others and a critical focus for collective action. For many, this solidarity crystallized further during the pandemic.

Conclusion

Erotic dance and stripping have performative and stage work elements that participants responding to the survey described as having a particular allure. Dancers described their peers as young women, often single mothers or students. They felt that the SEV licensing rules requiring evidence of right to work in the UK, as well as the need to be physically fit and engage in deep acting, meant that trafficking and coercion in the sector were rare. Rather, the principal harms articulated by participants were related to poor or exploitative management practices, which compromised both pay and safety. This resonates with the experiences of managed brothel workers in Chapter 5. It signals the potential for abuse when third parties are involved in the running of sex industry premises, particularly where the law is unclear, erratically enforced and stigma means that sex workers risk compromising their own position if they speak out.

A number of dancers identified explicitly as feminists and felt frustrated with the national and local discourse on SEVs. Their perception was that, on the one hand, women are reassured that they are never accountable for sexual violence and abuse; yet dancers felt they were indirectly charged as complicit with facilitating localized gender violence, by choosing to work in SEVs.

SEVs are a measure for how and what society problematizes in relation to gendered and sexual practices and how these are in turn understood in relation to patriarchal violence and abuse. Many critics of the stripping sector see SEVs as both an outcome and perpetuation of gender inequality. This is linked in turn to economic inequality. For the participants in this chapter, the economic exploitation of those working in precarious, poorly regulated and gig sectors is the primary issue. They believe that legal and financial security affords individuals greater power and choice over how they earn income and to articulate the workplace conditions that they should expect.

7

Sex Buyers

In the UK and around the world, it is mainly men who pay for sexual services. Beyond that, clients are diverse in age, occupation status and ethnicity; the latter often reflecting location (Birch and Ireland, 2015; Grov et al, 2014). In England and Wales, it is legal to pay for sex but not to solicit for sex on the street (Section 51A of the Sexual Offences Act 2003) or to pay for sex with someone who is coerced by a third party (Section 53A of the Sexual Offences Act 2003).

Existing academic research on paying for sex has focused on: classifying buying patterns and habits (for example, Månsson, 2004; Soothill and Sanders, 2005; Sanders, 2008); online sex buyer forums or 'punter sites' (for example, Katsulis, 2010; Carter et al, 2021); the relationship between sex purchase and masculinities (for example, Coy et al, 2007; Joseph and Black, 2012; Hammond and van Hooff, 2019) or power (for example, Monto and Milrod, 2020); and the role of intimacy, authenticity and a 'girlfriend experience' sought specifically by some buyers within paid sex transactions (for example, Huff, 2011; Milrod and Monto, 2012).

Fewer studies have looked at male clients who pay for sex with other men (for example, Grov et al, 2014; Tewksbury and Lapsey, 2017) and women who pay for sex with men and women (for example, Kingston et al, 2020; Caldwell and de Wit, 2021). Clients, like sex workers, may also identify as queer or non-binary, or pay for sex as part of a same- or mixed-gender couple. In the follow-up interviews to the Home Office survey, I asked all participants about both their experiences of paying for *and* selling sexual services and this is discussed briefly in this chapter.

The inclusion of sex buyer voices in the original Home Office report was criticized by some participants who felt that such work should focus only on sex workers. For example:

> They're your boyfriends and husbands, your brothers and dads, your sons, your co-workers. They're just men! And men are quite uninteresting. I think sex workers should be the focus of research on

sex work. I think the existing research too often focuses on talking about men and their motivations. (Female independent escort)

At the same time, I also received direct email correspondence from a small number of male buyers who were keen to ensure that their experience was included in the Home Office study and who were concerned that there was not a specific category in our survey for them to identify as 'clients'. In part, this may have related to concerns that a Nordic style model would be implemented following publication of the report. As a research team, we felt on balance that to understand the 'nature and prevalence' of the contemporary sex industry in England and Wales, it was important to include all voices. In theory, that could have included third party managers (on which research is scarce: for example, Farmer and Horowitz, 2013; Büschi, 2014), although none made contact, nor did we try to engage this group. We did however work with two key adult services websites who provided anonymized data and context for the online sex industry in the UK. I mention this discussion to mark the sensitivity and ethical challenges about who speaks on the sex industry and the responsibility for researchers that comes with presenting those different voices.

Participant narratives (original email interview)

In this section are presented longer narratives from Byron, Milton and Nathaniel, all men who have paid for sex regularly. The excerpts are followed by discussion, drawing in also brief quotes from other buyers who participated in the original research.

Byron's story (male sex buyer)

I started in my early 20s in the mid-eighties paying for an intimate service from a masseuse at a [name of city] massage parlour. Nowadays, I pay for an hour or so, probably once a month now, and I enjoy the experience of intimacy more so than just paying to have sex.

[The organization of appointments] depends on the type of sex workers. Sex workers, in my experience, who are independent can usually be contacted directly via email or by calling them. However, if the sex worker works at a third-party's flat or other establishment, then a maid will handle client calls and take bookings.

Independent (BDSM) Mistresses are contacted mainly through email. To stop time wasters, a deposit is required to secure an appointment via a bank transfer or an e-gift card. The other type of sex workers, who work at a third-party's property, are paid in cash. This is done as soon as the sex worker has introduced herself. I have not used escort agencies, but I think an agency requires credit card payment to secure an escort's booking to a hotel. Then I imagine a separate cash payment to the escort for intimate services to be provided.

I have seen, and continue to see, White and mainly British women. I have seen a wide range of ages from 20s to 40s over the years. I've seen sex workers at massage parlours. The women there were a mix of ages, different nationalities but mainly White British. That was back in the 80s, so this is probably a lot different now. I have also visited sex workers at third-party premises e.g. residential house. The type of sex worker mainly seen were early middle-aged, very ordinary, down to earth people. At this type of place, client turnover was brisk, and your time was limited with the sex worker. I stopped visiting this type of place when I spotted an advert by an independent worker living in [English city]. She was a very attractive, British White woman, well-educated and approx. mid 30s. She told me that she had a career in banking but never disclosed why she became a sex worker. She was expensive compared to what I had been paying up till then. Yet being with her was relaxing, entertaining and fun. Now the two sex workers I see regularly are both their mid to late 40s, White British. They are charming people whose company I enjoy by sharing meals, coffee and intimacy.

A few years ago, I began BDSM sessions – I think to escape my own reality. By relinquishing control, and placing my complete trust in the Mistress, was a method to reach a natural high. I was very fortunate to session with an experienced and highly regarded Mistress. Prior to our session, we had a long discussion that I found to be incredibly helpful and illuminating.

The main reason I began paying for sex was because I was a very unhappy, sexually frustrated young man. I suffered with a chronic lack of self-esteem and displayed an introvert behaviour. I felt unattractive to women and rarely approached them. Paying for sex at least gave me a brief respite from the mental anxiety and frustration. I didn't seek any professional help, but just dealt with it the best I could. I have continued to struggle to have meaningful, loving relationships all my adult life. So, I continue to pay for sex as it makes my life bearable, if not particularly happy.

The internet has changed the buying experience completely. It's so much easier at the click of a mouse or using a phone to find sex workers. Both sex workers and those seeking intimate services can register with [an adult service website]. From specific search filters of sex workers, you get a selection of those available in an area and services provided. Years ago – pre-internet – I would have to check personal classified ads in local papers. I also used other publications with a wider circulation in [name of city] that carried these types of ads e.g. [mentions three listings and classified newspapers]. In the mid-90s telephone boxes in major towns would be regularly covered inside by elaborate sex worker business cards that gave brief details about the worker and a number to call. A maid would answer the phone and usually read out a written, often exaggerated description of the sex worker and the fee, together with the general location. You were then told to call again when you reached a particular nearby street. On that call you were given the exact location.

[I will continue to pay for sex unless] sex work fees are increased beyond what I could afford, or I am unable to locate available sex workers. [I will pay as long as I am] fit and able because I enjoy it and as I've missed out on so much.

I have answered your survey as truthfully as I can. I am happy to answer any follow up questions if it helps. I am disturbed why the research has been commissioned and believe it's the first step to criminalise those people who sell and buy sex. I assume that the main factor driving this Parliamentary interest in sex work derives from the problems of sex trafficking into the country. This is an abominable crime which must be dealt with by the authorities.

However, if the ultimate plan for the greater good is to criminalise consenting adults, then I believe that this is wrong.

These so-called Parliamentary do-gooders are meddling in people's private lives. [...] A female sex worker consents to provide intimate services for an agreed fee to me. I consent to pay the agreed fee before the intimate service is provided. However, the key aspect for the meddlers to understand is that both parties – in the provision and receipt of sexual services – acknowledge and accept that consent can be revoked by either party at any time. Any situation where a sex worker or a client is forced to do anything against their will is obviously wrong and wrongdoers should be punished.

Milton's story (male sex buyer)

I was working in [an African city] in my early twenties. [...] There were virtually no single European girls, and it would have been inappropriate to have had a serious African girlfriend, so, on Saturday night I would go to [a particular] night club at around midnight, where there were lots of very pretty [local nationality] girls who would spend the night with me. [...] I only caught a relatively minor STD once, which was lucky. As I was leaving, the existence and dangers of HIV were becoming widely known. [...]

Returning to work in the UK and Europe, I had a succession of girlfriends and finally got married [a decade or so] ago. Only since getting married have I started to see escorts again as I crave the variety. Whilst single, with a steady girlfriend, I was always on the lookout for other intimate opportunities which sometimes developed into relationships. Since being married, I do not want to cheat on my wife with other relationships so, although seeing escorts is strictly cheating, I consider it to be less so. Typically, I will see a provider around once a month on average now.

In the past, my purchased services have been fairly conventional but in the last few years I have started to explore some fetishes, and especially enjoy being dominated by attractive young women.

There is [an adult services] website that now dominates the industry. [...] It has a very useful search facility which allows you to select age range, proximity to postcode and a menu of other filters to find what you are looking for. Its most valuable feature is the feedback punters can give (if they have booked an appointment through the site) so the number of positive feedbacks in relation to the date the profile was registered is a great way to find a good service. [...]

I have never used an agency to find an escort, I prefer to find independent ladies, although I'm not convinced that all the ladies on [the adult services website] are truly independent.

I have tried [sugar dating websites] in the hope of finding a discreet regular arrangement but most of the ladies are either thinly disguised escorts expecting to charge a premium over escort prices or ladies who want a real relationship. [...] It's actually hard to find a student or single mother who could really do with some financial help who is willing to be intimate with just a selected number of gentlemen, maybe even just one, with the understanding that it's just a financial arrangement.

[Arrangement] is almost always by telephone, calling the mobile number on the website. Most escorts insist on the caller number not being hidden, which is a sensible safety precaution.

I normally put the money in an unsealed envelope. On arrival, escorts generally ask for how long and they tell me the price (which is almost always the same as that advertised) and I give them the envelope. Being polite and showing respect and consideration has always assured me of a good service and pleasant interaction. [...]

My favourite ladies are [nationality] – they all appear to be highly educated, very good at pleasing a man, full of fun and brilliant at making you think they would really like to see you again!

I would say that most of the ladies are not gold diggers – they are trying to earn money to help pay for their education, their children and/or their family. I personally have the greatest respect for their motivations, and I regret that the profession is still regarded with suspicion and is stigmatised in the UK.

From my experience talking to escorts, it is rare for them to have successful relationships with men whilst they are escorting. [...] I must confess that I am unaware of any of my friends and acquaintances who pay for these services. I feel sure that some do, but it's so important that it remains confidential, and I think many men would be embarrassed to admit that they do.

[The benefits are that] it is generally good value for money and one can explore interests which are not favoured by one's partner. It is also discreet and it's a business relationship which doesn't overhang the time paid for. Also, I can visit younger ladies with whom I could never see for sex any other way. [...]

We need to lighten up about the whole profession. Largely, the police are sensible and ignore it all. The danger is that government will decide they need to take action. Sorry to say, but the world works fine in almost every respect until government takes action – almost every change they make is stupid as they are so far isolated from reality. It is crucial that there is a quiet but systematic process to verify that ladies are working independently, or at least in an agreed structure for their mutual benefit.

[In terms of the challenges and harms] for service providers, the sensible ones do it for a limited time only. I think it can be lonely, stressful and difficult to return to a life after. For clients, there is a danger that they become obsessed and struggle with normal relationships. Overall, I think the mental health issues far outweigh the physical health risks.

Nathaniel's story (male sex buyer)

I started buying sexual services [in recent years]. My wife and I had not had sex for over a decade. I don't want her to do something she doesn't want to do (for whatever reason), so I proposed I see escorts as I don't see why one person can unilaterally end another's sex life without at least some discussion. She was not happy at the time, but I think she is now relieved she doesn't have to do it anymore. It's not a perfect solution by any means: it's certainly not what I signed up for. But for me, it's about intimacy and human contact, not something you can get from pornography. I usually purchase a 'girlfriend experience'. I enjoy the intimacy I have not experienced with my wife [of many] years. I found [an adult services website] by searching on the internet and I use that for all my meets.

I have a budget so as not to adversely affect family finances. This enables me to make bookings once a month. But this year, I have been fortunate enough to have had the money to make bookings about once every 2 weeks, due to investments and bonuses.

[I use an adult services website] for searching and making bookings and a [sex buyer site] for cross referencing other people who may have seen a girl, just to ensure I am not in danger of being conned or short changed.

I usually book a couple of weeks in advance. I follow the procedure as laid out in the girl's profile (usually a message through the [adult services website] system), but sometimes they prefer a text or a phone call, if they want to speak to you beforehand.

I have always paid cash to the girl in person. If we've never met before that's usually up front at the beginning of a meet to reassure her I will not 'do a runner' – but if we have met before it can be at the end.

Obviously, I cannot always know why these women do what they do, so I always try to see educated British women so there are no language issues and so I can satisfy myself they are not being pimped or forced in any way.

If I can, I try to see girls who say they are part-time, as this can mean that they are in it at least partially for the sex, as well as the money. I have met many women who do this work part-time. Housewives, students (one who was paying for driving lessons), nurses, someone who was saving for a house deposit.

My tastes are quite vanilla. I have bought intimate massages and the arrangements and demographics tend to be very similar, though there are often restrictions on what a client can and can't do. One time I saw a girl and we just slept in each other's arms: it was lovely and everything I always wanted with my wife.

I do not know any other buyers but, reading the [sex buyer website], there do seem to be a lot of men with a similar demographic (age, social class) and similar experiences (intimacy free marriage) to me.

I never really had a very interesting or exciting sex life, I had only three sexual partners prior to taking up this 'hobby', so the variety is a big factor. I can try different things with different girls which I had never done before. It is easier, simpler and more convenient than the dating scene (which I have always struggled with), and it is relatively transparent. The girl knows what I want; I know what she wants: there is no power play or subtext.

I think the challenges of sex work are probably seeing clients who aren't physically attractive or who do not possess the correct level of social skills required to find women any other way. The client may be old or disabled or have issues with hygiene, both body and oral, as well as social stigma. The risks are from the clients, I would guess. Violence; clients pushing boundaries; trying to get the girl to do things she doesn't want to do; or aggressively trying to get a discount; STIs; outing by clients.

The harms are becoming jaded through overwork. I have heard some girls talk of loneliness.

Discussion of first interviews

In this section, I discuss both the narratives presented in the previous section and draw on the wider first interview and survey data. The buyers presented here have slightly different reasons for paying for sex, which fit the existing typology work outlined in the introduction. Byron said he 'struggle[d] to have meaningful, loving relationships all [his] adult life' and started paying for sex in his mid-twenties to try to assuage feelings of isolation and frustration. Milton also engaged in commercial sex early, initially as a young man working internationally. He married in recent years and recommended meeting escorts, on average monthly. Milton said that, in his previous relationships, he did not pay for sex but was always 'on the lookout for other intimate opportunities' and so is interested in sexual variety. Nathaniel was married and his wife had not wanted a sexual relationship 'for over a decade'. He discussed his decision to pay for sex with his wife and, although he said she was not happy, he suspected she now felt 'relieved', albeit he noted this is 'not a perfect solution'. All three buyers to some extent sought companionship and intimacy, as well as sex, but particularly Nathaniel and Byron. More recently, Byron had moved into exploring fantasy and found this experience emotionally therapeutic.

Milton positioned himself as both personally and sexually explorative – having lived and worked around the world – and his longer narrative recounts his experiences with women of different nationalities. He was both flattered by the attention of women, but also cognisant that 'paying attention' and 'appearing interested' is part of the labour of sex work: what Julia O'Connell Davidson (1998) terms the 'fiction of mutuality'. Relatedly, he talked also about his desire to provide pleasure, which reflects Katsulis' observation of male buyers that 'the giving of sexual pleasure to others [may be] part of the pleasure being purchased' (2010, p 224).

All three buyers were aware of the harms of commercial sex, with Nathaniel providing a list which matched many provided by sex workers in their interviews. The respondents felt the risks were primarily emotional and psychological and were keen to communicate throughout their narratives that they paid for sex responsibly. Similarly, this survey respondent argued:

I simply do not understand that some people and some groups argue that the customers of sex workers are guilty of violence or exploitation. I know that the Crown Prosecution Service's guidance on prostitution comes in the section headed 'Violence against Women and Girls (VAWG)'; the guidance explains that it is there 'due to its gendered nature'. But this does not mean that prostitution is violence, simply that it is dealt with under that heading by the CPS as the majority of cases that come to their attention involve women and often violence. (Male sex buyer)

Byron, Milton and Nathaniel felt strongly that the consensual selling and paying for sexual services should not be criminalized. They planned to continue doing so, as long as the law facilitated.

Participant reflections (second email interview)

This section presents follow-up interviews with Milton and Byron: Nathaniel was unavailable by the time I conducted second interviews in spring 2021.

Byron's reflection (male sex buyer)

I started paying for sex at 24, but I had been considering it months beforehand. It was not something I particularly wanted to do, and I hoped I would have a relationship with a woman, just like most men my age. I felt guilty that I could even think of paying for sex, but by 24 I felt I had no alternative. I was sexually frustrated, with chronic low self-esteem and prone to irrational outbursts of anger. As I remember, after my first time, I was just happy to have been intimate with a woman. It definitely boosted my morale and made me feel more of a man. Over the next few years of paying for sex, I tended to see particular women on a more regular basis and this semi-familiarity with them gave me the illusion of a girlfriend experience.

Simply put, COVID-19 has been an unmitigated disaster for me. I am extremely vulnerable to the virus as I have a transplant and take immune suppressants. I will be vaccinated, but exactly how effective it will be for someone like myself is still largely unknown by medical authorities. I live alone and have rarely left my home in the last year, due to shielding. I haven't been with a sex worker since 2019 and have no plans to do so for the foreseeable future, due to fear of infection.

Thank you for inviting me to contribute to your research. It has been the only time I've disclosed to anyone that I've paid for sex. It's been a challenge, but I'm pleased to have made a small contribution to your important research. I always take an interest in any discussion / debate about the sex industry. I can offer my opinion on a couple of aspects that particularly interest me.

The type of physical and emotional support sex workers can provide to some men who are e.g., disabled, lonely, elderly, psychological issues etc. is not usually acknowledged. It is, however, an important aspect ignored (or they're not aware) by many Parliamentarians, media, and miscellaneous interest groups, when the sex industry comes under scrutiny. Men, who pay for sex, are mostly criticised and ridiculed and accused of exploiting women. That's the standard generalisation often trotted out. For the types of men described (myself included), sex workers can provide essential support. Therefore, the imposition of social distancing, and consequentially its huge adverse effect on sex work, has probably exacerbated existing mental health issues many of these men may already experience.

Personally speaking, paying for sex has helped me cope with my largely disappointing, lonely life. Not being able to see a sex worker during this last year – and not knowing when this may be possible again – has added to the mental and emotional stress I've suffered throughout this wretched COVID-19 crisis.

I have also read about possible legislation based on the 'Nordic Model' which many sex workers are against. I understand it also seeks to criminalise those who pay for sex and, if true, that's very unfair. I have always been respectful towards every sex worker I met, and this was usually reciprocated. As far as I'm concerned, we are consenting adults and should be treated as such by the law.

Milton's reflection (male sex buyer)

I am happy with what I wrote. I hope it was helpful.

Since lockdown, I have not visited any service providers as I can imagine they would be especially vulnerable to COVID-19 infection. I have helped out two of my favourite providers with money during the lockdown – they must all be struggling for income at the moment, although I am stunned to see how many escorts continue to offer appointments at the moment. I would argue that escorts should be prioritised for the COVID inoculation, for the benefit of the mental health of the nation. I have spent more time on social media and signed up to several [content subscription service] online providers.

I am aware that the length of the [2019 Home Office] report had to be kept short, and that the emphasis needed to be about service providers than customers. Perhaps the book will have room to re-address this balance.

Discussion of second interviews

Milton's buying habits have shifted online since the pandemic. Like Cordelia in Chapter 3, he is surprised to see some independent escorts continuing to offer services. While it is possible that, in common with other members of the public, some sex workers broke lockdown rules through choice rather than necessity, it also visibilizes the perception gap between the professional and positive profile of escorts, as seen by their clients, and the underlying financial, legal and social precarity that many experienced once lockdown began. For those without access to savings, state or familial support, work was the only option.

For Byron, COVID-19 has had a significant impact. He has been shielding due to health vulnerabilities and had throughout his life relied on paid sex as the principal lifeline in negotiating long-term feelings of isolation. His description of the value of commercial sex for him in providing personal connection echoes the accounts of some sex workers in Chapters 3 and 4. The lockdown experience has confirmed his view that consensual paid sex should not be criminalized.

Milton would have liked to have seen more coverage of clients in the original Home Office report, though recognizes that there was a constraint on word count overall and the emphasis was rightly on sex workers. For Byron, the process of engaging in research, rather than the final output, has been valuable:

> It has been the only time I've disclosed to anyone that I've paid for sex. It's been a challenge, but I'm pleased to have made a small contribution to your important research.

In earlier correspondence, Nathaniel also spoke of the difficulty he experienced reflecting on and writing his responses to the first interview – and in ultimately pressing 'send'.

Sellers' experience of paying for sex

As part of the original email interviews, I asked buyers about their experience and attitudes towards selling sex themselves and I asked sellers about their experience and feelings about paying for sexual services. Many sellers found it hard to imagine a situation where they would need to pay (similarly, one male buyer joked whether any woman would pay 'an overweight, bald, middle-aged man!'). Some sellers were however open in principle to the idea, particularly if it was something specific they wanted to experience. Others spoke of already paying dancers and adult content providers as a way of recognizing and valuing their work. A small number had paid for escorts, male or female, and one female worker recalled occasionally paying for other women when high on drugs, but for company and someone to talk to, not for sex. A couple of male sex buyers disclosed having also experimented temporarily selling sexual services to other men (although their paid sex history had been with female sex workers). For others, paid sex was problematic, because it resonated with their own conflicted experience:

> I would find it difficult because I know what a difficult process it can be for the worker at times, so I'd find it hard to potentially be a part of that. (Independent female sex worker)

A small number of sex worker respondents had found their paid sex experience either underwhelming ('I didn't choose well' (female independent sex worker)) or, indeed, abusive – for example:

> Yes, I had a session with a [type of masseur]. It was the worst sexual experience of my life. Later I learned that this guy was [convicted previously for assault]. Now he's running a [type of massage venue] and posing as an expert in the field. Revolting. (Female erotic masseur)

Both these participants, however, said they would consider paying again in future. A final reason given by respondents was to see what it felt like being the client and to learn from others' practice.

Conclusion

While a small proportion of women do pay for sex, the majority of sex buyers are male. They are socially diverse, and they articulate different motives for engaging in the commercial sex sector in addition to, or in place of, non-commercial sex. The Home Office report (Hester et al, 2019, p 23) classified motivations as personal, practical and sexual: these were not mutually exclusive and could shift over time. In common with contemporary consumption practices, paying for sex may be understood as an exercise of economic power, and may also reflect other power relations of gender, age or nationality, for example. Some sex workers may also exert power within a commercial sex transaction, due for example to education, economic security or age. In this way, the exercise of power does not always link to violence, although, in some contexts, it may link to harm.

The buyers who shared their stories in this chapter were keen to underline that they engage in consensual paid sex, which they do not believe should attract criminal sanction, and that they reject and condemn coercion and trafficking, which should. In terms of coercion, I have written elsewhere (Mulvihill, 2019) about the difference between *interpersonal* coercion (threats, force or blackmail exercised over an individual by another person or group) and *structural* coercion (an individual feeling compelled to sell sex to cope with acute economic circumstances or social discrimination). I argue that there is the potential for harm in paying for sex with individuals in the second as well as the first group. But it is not clear that buyers can be held individually and criminally accountable for structural coercion, unless the consequences, in the minds of most reasonable people, demonstrably interfere with decision-making and autonomy: for example, where sex workers are disoriented through substance misuse or are clearly distressed or withdrawn. Paying does not and should not buy consent: but it may do so in conditions of inequality (and some will argue that the buying and selling of sex occurs only within inequality). For the independent sex workers in this book, payment is for a defined and bounded service which they offer, and with which the buyer should comply.

The buyers who participated in the Home Office research all agreed in principle that mutuality should guide law on commercial sex, as it does in non-commercial sexual relationships. They felt too that public policy should be focused on tackling structural coercion.

8

Reflection

Participant feedback

In this final chapter, I describe the process of seeking feedback on individual chapters from each participant before going on to reflect on the methodological implications of the book overall. I acknowledge also the limitations and absences.

Sixteen participants whose first email interviews were quoted at length in the book were contacted to provide feedback on their chapter. This is two fewer than the original 18 who agreed to participate in the book (see Figure 2.1) and is because one participant's first – and only – interview was used only for brief excerpts and another first interview was provided by a participant who gave permission for their story to be included but was unable to engage in the follow-up interview or review process.

Fourteen out of the 16 participants contacted provided feedback on their chapters. Ten participants requested edits: these ranged from spotting small typos to minor redaction or amendment to their interviews. These were principally to preserve anonymity but also where participants wanted to clarify or edit something that they had said. In three cases, I amended my commentary following an interview edit, though not in terms of the substantive point being made. Apart from this, there were no requests to change the discussion sections. Four participants were happy with the chapter as it stood.

Almost all participants explicitly welcomed the chapter review process, because it maintained their influence over the presentation and discussion of their story. For example:

> Honestly, I think this is really important as it gives us a further voice to add in this editorial stage.

> I think it's great that you're letting people review these chapters before they go to publication. I am mostly happy with mine [but could I just take out X and Y as] I feel like there's a few too many identifying details.

I did definitely appreciate being able to read the chapter and be given the opportunity to respond before publication; it would feel too much like an unknown quantity to not have had and taken that opportunity.

In reviewing their narrative, participants were keen to emphasize where they experienced particular privileges (for example related to education or gender) and recognize that other sex workers may experience the sex industry differently. Relatedly, two participants were alert to how readers of the book may appropriate an isolated incident recounted in their narrative as evidence for systemic and widespread harm: this led to two small edits to reinforce the specific context for their comment. This demonstrates how some participants felt the dual responsibility of representing themselves, but also their peers and the sex industry more widely. This was less self-censorship and more a high level of reflexivity about how their narratives would be read and interpreted, given their long-standing and often negative experiences of being spoken about by others, in the media and public debate.

Reflections on method

McCoyd and Shdaimah's (2007, p 347) work identifies three reasons why participants get involved in research:

(1) the validation of being understood and of having one's story heard in full without judgment; (2) the chance to have one's story joined with others in such a way as to create a 'voice' on a topic of shared experiences, and (3) the knowledge that findings will be published and communicated to providers, policymakers, and the public.

The second interviews suggest that the participants were broadly content with the Home Office report, in particular the use of direct quotes from sex workers. They recognized the constraints of the report format and saw benefits and limitations in the decision to take a broad definition of the sex industry. However, the approach in this book of giving more in-depth focus to different groups, of presenting lengthy narratives and of asking participants to read and exert some editorial control on the chapter drafts did, I believe, strengthen further the sense of research as a validating process:

I'm so touched that you have printed my story.

The chapter looks great, and I'm really glad our voices have been put to the forefront!

The opportunity to read each other's stories also enabled participants to 'cross-check' with others presented in their chapter:

> It's been very interesting reading the responses from the other sex workers you interviewed in the chapter: we all seem to align on the majority of key points, which has reassured me that a lot of us are on the same page.

> Interesting to read the differences and similarities between the three buyers. I like that all three show a similar respect and gratitude towards service providers.

In terms of McCoyd and Shdaimah's (2007) third motivation, that the knowledge produced will be published and communicated to those who have the power to effect change: this is more difficult. The 2019 Home Office report has not led to any significant policy change in relation to the sex industry – although it may have halted or delayed planned change: we do not know. As I outline in Chapter 2, it was concern about how those involved in the sex industry are already subject to regular government, parliamentary, NGO and academic inquiry – in other words: *have already spoken many times* – that led me to ask the participants if I could publish those collected interviews in full.

In relation to soliciting feedback on chapter drafts, Thomas (2017, p 39) suggests that where research is concerned particularly in 'ensuring accurate representation of participants' perspectives or experiences ... [then] selective use of member checks may be justified'. Beyond this, he is sceptical about how giving participants control over what is said makes the research more valid or credible, in methodological terms, or indeed how authors should negotiate conflicting feedback. For me, the format of reproducing long narratives in this book meant that open collaboration with participants was critical: these were *their* stories. Visibilizing the reflection and review process also disrupts the notion that academic research or policy reports are straightforward summaries of what was said or agreed. Rather, such texts are always contested and unfinished – what Bakhtin described as *dialogic* (2004 [1986]) – and this perspective is consistent with Tracy's (2010) preference for 'member reflections' rather than 'member checks', described in Chapter 2. In this research, some participants requested to tweak slightly their first or second interview, to clarify or reinterpret a point they had made. It could be argued that this is 'tampering with the data'. However, I came to see this very differently and it links to the discussion in Chapter 2 about recognizing the constructed nature of our narratives (Gergen, 1994; Çalişkan, 2018); how all stories are selected and partial.

Chandler (1990) describes autobiographical writing as a 'healing art': while there is therapeutic value, life story writing also documents who we (thought we) were then, and that can change over time. I realized through the process of writing this book that, in academic research, we need to be careful about keeping that shifting identity in mind and being careful not to over-infer from participant accounts given at one point in time. The current cultural trend, spurred by social media, is to hold people to account for 'what they said then' as if views and identities are preserved in aspic over time. Even in two years, and particularly due to the extraordinary circumstances of COVID-19, the participant reflections record how all of us can shift in our identity and ideas over time.

> It feels slightly strange reading back on the answers I gave, despite it not being that long ago. I think some of my language has changed.

> Realising that I spent several years as a coerced young person is difficult to read, knowing it is my own story, but also a relief to realise how much I have changed and grown since then.

In Chapter 3, Blake identifies a 'defensiveness' in their first interview that they think is common to sex workers who are 'very used to seeing a narrative of our work as tragedy and pathology'. It is likely that the context of the first interviews, where participants were responding to government-funded research and were aware of policy discussions about the viability of a Nordic-style model in England and Wales or a ban on adult service websites, meant some responded with a more strident and Panglossian account of sex work. It may be a more selective story told necessarily in a context where narratives are under constant scrutiny by others seeking to 'score political goals', as Titiania says in Chapter 5. But it may also have been some participants' authentic, straight-from-the-hip experience. The problem is that the hostile tone of many debates on the sex industry has made open reflection by sex workers difficult. Opinions and experiences, good and bad interwoven, are often not listened to in the round. Instead, particular threads are isolated and pulled out as evidence.

Through history, narrative and life stories – fictional, factual and in combination – have always been celebrated for their insight into the human condition. As Gergen (1994) argued, they are accounts constructed by individuals to make sense of life. In postmodern times, our welcome embrace of critique and plurality has also perhaps engendered an unhelpful cynicism. In Chapter 3, one survey respondent and former escort said, 'ask them when they finally leave the scene, and you will have a different outcome from their responses' – implying that participants would be 'more truthful', which is assumed to equate to 'more negative' about their experience. The second interviews enabled participants to be more reflective and most had either left or had periods absent from 'the scene' due to the pandemic.

While for some, and consistent with my earlier comment that our identity and opinions may develop over time (particularly during such a profound social event as a pandemic), their view of sex work had shifted slightly. For a couple, including Emilia in Chapter 5, they had started to or confirmed a reassessment of their experience as damaging – others had not. Their views were essentially unchanged. It should not be assumed that all former sex workers with sufficient passage of time and emotional honesty will come to see their experience as harmful and identify as 'survivors'. And nor should sex workers' reflections – whether damning or celebratory – be dismissed pejoratively as 'their truth' when they do not align with a particular political position. Most of the participants in this group remain neutral-positive about sex work. Such reflections will always be informed by why and how someone enters sex work in the first place, their socio-economic and wellbeing status and their experiences while involved.

But are the participants in this book 'average' sex workers? There is no 'average', but the sample does not sufficiently represent migrant workers, or those from Black African, Black Caribbean, South Asian, East Asian or Mixed Heritage groups, or those trafficked or coerced by another individual or group into selling sex. These are significant limitations. Similar issues were acknowledged in the 2019 Home Office report, and it was recognized that some of the methods, as well as being funded by the UK Home Office, may have mitigated against the inclusion of those with insecure migrant status, or who were not active online or engaged with support services, or who would be deterred by the literacy and time requirements of completing written questions. Indeed, the survey used for the 2019 Home Office report did not ask for demographic data (such as gender, age, nationality or ethnicity) from participants, because of the concern that this may discourage them from responding. However, it was possible often to infer some of this from respondents who described, unprompted, both their own context and that of individuals and peers in the industry.

The experience of migrant workers and those from Black African, Black Caribbean, South Asian, East Asian or Mixed Heritage groups are captured within other British studies of the sex industry (see, for example, Sagar et al, 2011; Sanders et al, 2017; Bowen, 2021) and other academic researchers, including Professor Nicola Mai, Dr Katie Cruz and Professor Vanessa Munro, have written on the intersections of citizenship status, migration law and sex work in the UK. In the past decade, NGOs have tended to produce and commission much of the research both on migrant and minoritized groups and those who have been trafficked or exploited, including most recently in relation to the impact of the COVID-19 pandemic (see, for example, Changing Lives, 2020; National Ugly Mugs (NUM) and Femmedaemonium, 2020; Thiara and Roy, 2020; Beyond the Streets and the Joint Public Issues Team, 2021; Fedorkó et al, 2021).

We do not know exactly the proportions of different social identities and contexts of individuals who work in the sex industry. The sample in this book may privilege those who are more articulate, autonomous and active within the sex worker community: this is true. Furthermore, this book focuses only on England and Wales, so caution should be exercised in seeking to extrapolate and apply insights to other jurisdictions. At the same time, the experiences of these participants are likely to represent a significant share of those currently or recently engaged in the indoor and independent sectors of the sex industry in England and Wales. In addition, as their stories show, aspects of 'privilege' are relational and may shift over time.

Endings and beginnings

Fenton, as you may remember from Chapter 4, has been an important critical voice through this project. In providing feedback on his chapter, he reiterated his concerns about academics speaking for sex workers as consistent with the exploitation and silencing of sex workers and other marginalized groups through time. To this end, he called for a 'Sex Workers' history, under our own community authorship'. I think – I hope – there is a role for academics in standing within and standing back, to produce useful knowledge for social change. However, it is critical too that people are resourced to write and direct the presentation of their own and their collective stories. Otherwise, their experiences may fall between the pages written by those with power to hold the pen.

In the poem 'Little Gidding' (1942), T.S. Eliot writes about arriving where we started and knowing the place for the first time. This captures well the experience of research. No matter how many years spent studying an issue, the initial landscape keeps receding further and further back, revealing a much more complex picture than first seen. You arrive eventually at the start, but with different eyes and expectations. The narratives of the participants in this book – and many like them – will continue, documented or not. Their stories, among many, unfolding over the contested terrain of the sex industry.

Notes

Chapter 1

[1] Professor Marianne Hester was Principal Investigator; Dr Andrea Matolcsi, Dr Alba Lanau Sanchez, Sarah-Jane Walker and I were Co-investigators. However, please note that any views expressed in this book are my own and do not, or may not, reflect the views of the Co-investigators or the Principal Investigator.

[2] There are three legal jurisdictions in the UK: Scotland; Northern Ireland; and England and Wales. The remit of the 2019 Home Office report was 'England and Wales', and therefore the legal context outlined in selected sections in this book also refers to this jurisdiction, unless otherwise specified.

Chapter 5

[1] Possibly referring here to the All-Party Parliamentary Group (APPG) on Prostitution and the Sex Trade 2014. The Home Office report was actually a recommendation of the Home Affairs Committee (2016, Conclusion, para 16) (see pp 3–4, this volume).

References

All-Party Parliamentary Group on Prostitution and the Global Sex Trade, 2014. *Shifting the Burden: Inquiry to Assess the Operation of the Current Legal Settlement on Prostitution in England and Wales*. London: APPG. Available at: https://appgprostitution.files.wordpress.com/2014/04/shifting-the-burden.pdf [accessed 11 March 2022].

Bakhtin, M.M., 2004 [1986]. *Speech Genres and Other Late Essays*. 9th reprint. Translated from Russian by V.W. McGee. 1986. Edited by C. Emerson and M. Holquist. Austin: University of Texas Press.

Baral, S.D., Friedman, M.R., Geibel, S., Rebe, K., Bozhinov, B., Diouf, D., Sabin, K., Holland, C.E., Chan, R. and Cáceres, C.F., 2015. Male sex workers: Practices, contexts, and vulnerabilities for HIV acquisition and transmission. *Lancet*, 385(9964), 260–273.

Barry, K.L., 1984. *Sexual Slavery*. New York: New York University Press.

Baum, F., MacDougall, C. and Smith, D., 2006. Participatory action research. *Journal of Epidemiology and Public Health*, 60(10), 854–857.

Belle de Jour, 2007. *The Intimate Adventures of a London Call Girl*. New York: Grand Central Publishing.

Bergman, M.M., 2010. On concepts and paradigms in mixed methods research. *Journal of Mixed Methods Research*, 4(3), 171–175.

Beyond the Gaze, 2015–2018. *The Working Practices, Regulation and Safety of Internet-based Sex Work in the UK* [online]. Available at: https://www.beyond-the-gaze.com/ [accessed 11 March 2022].

Beyond the Streets and The Joint Public Issues Team, 2021. *The Impact of Covid-19 on Women who Sell Sex or are Sexually Exploited*. London: Beyond the Streets. Available at: https://beyondthestreets.org.uk/wp-content/uploads/2021/05/The-impact-of-Covid-19-on-women-who-sell-sex-or-are-sexually-exploited.pdf [accessed 11 March 2022].

Birch, P. and Ireland, J.L., 2015. Men procuring sexual services from women: Everyman or peculiar man? *The Journal of Forensic Practice*, 17(1), 13–20.

Birt, L., Scott, S., Cavers, D., Campbell, C. and Walter, F., 2016. Member checking: A tool to enhance trustworthiness or merely a nod to validation? *Qualitative Health Research*, 26(13), 1802–1811.

Bowen, R., 2021. *Work, Money and Duality: Trading Sex as a Side Hustle.* Bristol: Policy Press.

Brown, K., Cull, M. and Hubbard, P., 2010. The diverse vulnerabilities of lesbian, gay, bisexual and trans sex workers in the UK. In: K. Hardy, S. Kingston and T. Sanders (eds), *New Sociologies of Sex Work.* London: Routledge, pp 197–212.

Burns, E., 2010. Developing email interview practices in qualitative research. *Sociological Research Online*, 15(4), 1–12.

Büschi, E., 2014. Sex work and violence: Focusing on managers in the indoor sex industry. *Sexualities*, 17(5–6), 724–741.

Caldwell, H. and de Wit, J., 2021. Women's experiences buying sex in Australia: Egalitarian powermoves. *Sexualities*, 24(4), 549–573.

Çalişkan, G., 2018. *Conducting Narrative Inquiry in Sociological Research: Reflections from Research on Narratives of Everyday Encounters.* London: SAGE Publications.

Capous-Desyllas, M., 2013. Representations of sex workers' needs and aspirations: A case for arts-based research. *Sexualities*, 16(7), 772–787.

Capous-Desyllas, M., 2014. Using Photovoice with sex workers: The power of art, agency and resistance. *Qualitative Social Work*, 13(4), 477–501.

Carbonero, M.A. and Garrido, M.G., 2018. Being like your girlfriend: Authenticity and the shifting borders of intimacy in sex work. *Sociology*, 52(2), 384–399.

Carrier-Moisan, M-E., 2020. *Gringo Love: Stories of Sex Tourism in Brazil.* Toronto: University of Toronto Press.

Carter, P., Gee, M., McIlhone, H., Lally, H. and Lawson, R., 2021. Comparing manual and computational approaches to theme identification in online forums: A case study of a sex work special interest community. *Methods in Psychology*, 5. https://doi.org/10.1016/j.metip.2021.100065

Chandler, M.R., 1990. A healing art: Therapeutic dimensions of autobiography. *a/b: Auto/Biography Studies*, 5(1), 4–14.

Changing Lives, 2020. *Nowhere to Turn: Sexual Violence among Women Selling Sex and Experiencing Sexual Exploitation during Covid-19.* Gateshead: Changing Lives. Available at: https://www.changing-lives.org.uk/wp-content/uploads/2020/10/Nowhere-To-Turn-FINAL-REPORT.pdf [Accessed 11 March 2022].

Chowdhury, R., 2006. 'Outsiders' and identity reconstruction in the sex workers' movement in Bangladesh. *Sociological Spectrum*, 26(3), 335–357.

Chu, C.S.K., 2018. *Compensated Dating: Buying and Selling Sex in Cyberspace.* Singapore: Palgrave Macmillan.

Coy, M., Horvath, M. and Kelly, L., 2007. *'It's just like going to the supermarket': Men Buying Sex in East London.* Report for Safe Exit. London: Child and Woman Abuse Studies Unit, London Metropolitan University.

Crofts, T., 2014. Regulation of the Male Sex Industry. In: V. Minichello and J. Scott (eds), *Male Sex Work and Society*. New York: Columbia University Press, Ch 7.

Cunningham, S., Scoular, J., Pitcher, J., Sanders, T., Campbell, R., Hill, K., Valentine-Chase, M., Melissa, C., Aydin, Y. and Hamer, R., 2018. Behind the screen: Commercial sex, digital spaces and working online. *Technology in Society*, 53, 47–54.

De Castro Leal, D., Strohmayer, A. and Krüger, M., 2021. *On Activism and Academia: Reflecting Together and Sharing Experiences Among Critical Friends.* CHI '21, 8–13 May, Yokohama, Japan.

Delacoste, F. and Alexander, P., 2001. *Sex Work: Writings by Women in the Sex Industry*, 2nd edition. Minneapolis: Cleis Press.

Dennis, B.K., 2014. Understanding participant experiences: Reflections of a novice research participant. *International Journal of Qualitative Methods*, 13(1), 395–410.

Dewey, S., 2011a. *Neon Wasteland: On Love, Motherhood, and Sex Work in a Rust Belt Town.* Berkeley: University of California Press.

Dewey, S., 2011b. Demystifying sex work and sex workers. *Wagadu: A Journal of Transnational Women's and Gender Studies*, 8. Available at: https://sites.cortland.edu/wagadu/archive/demystifying-sex-work-and-sex-workers/ [accessed 11 March 2022].

Dewey, S., Orchard, T. and Harris, K., 2018. Shared precarities and maternal subjectivities: Navigating motherhood and child custody loss among North American women in street-based sex work. *Ethos: Journal of the Society for Psychological Anthropology*, 46(1), 27–48.

D'Ippoliti, C. and Botti, F., 2017. Sex work among trans people: Evidence from southern Italy. *Feminist Economics*, 23(3), 77–109.

Ditmore, M., Levy., A. and Willman, A., 2010. *Sex Work Matters: Exploring Money, Power, and Intimacy in the Sex Industry*. London and New York: Zed Books.

Eliot, T.S., 1942. *Little Gidding*. London: Faber & Faber.

Farmer, A. and Horowitz, A.W., 2013. Prostitutes, pimps, and brothels: Intermediaries, information, and market structure in prostitution markets. *Southern Economic Journal*, 79(3), 513–528.

Fedorkó, B., Stevenson, L. and Macioti, P.G., 2021. Sex workers on the frontline: An abridged version of the original ICRSE report: 'The role of sex worker rights groups in providing support during the COVID-19 crisis in Europe'. *Global Public Health*, DOI: 10.1080/17441692.2021.1945124

Freire, P., 1970 [1996]. *Pedagogy of the Oppressed*. London: Penguin Books.

Gee, C., 2011. *Hooked: Confessions of a London Call Girl*. Edinburgh: Mainstream Publishing.

Gergen, K.J., 1994. *Realities and Relationships: Soundings in Social Construction*. Cambridge, MA: Harvard University Press.

Gorman v Standen, Palace Clarke v Standen (1964) 48 Cr App R 30.

Grov, C., Wolff, M., Smith, M.D., Koken, J. and Parsons, J.T., 2014. Male clients of male escorts: Satisfaction, sexual behavior, and demographic characteristics. *Journal of Sex Research*, 51(7), 827–837.

Hammersley, M., 1992. *What's Wrong with Ethnography?* London: Routledge.

Hammond, N. and van Hooff, J., 2019. "This is me, this is what I am, I am a man": The masculinities of men who pay for sex with women. *The Journal of Sex Research*, 57(5), 650–663.

Heath, S.B., 1986. Taking a cross-cultural look at narratives. In: F. Kuecker (ed), *Topics in Language Disorders*. Rockville: Aspen Publishers, pp 84–94.

Hershberger, P.E. and Kavanaugh, K., 2017. Comparing appropriateness and equivalence of email interviews to phone interviews in qualitative research on reproductive decisions. *Applied Nursing Research*, 37, 50–54.

Hester, M., Mulvihill, N., Matolcsi, A., Lanau Sanchez, A., and Walker, S-J., 2019. *The Nature and Prevalence of Prostitution and Sex Work in England and Wales*. London: Home Office. Available at: https://www.gov.uk/gov ernment/publications/nature-of-prostitution-and-sex-work-in-england-and-wales [accessed 18 May 2021].

Hochschild, A., 1993. *The Managed Heart: Commercialization of Human Feeling*. Berkeley: University of California Press.

Hom, K.A. and Woods, S.J., 2013. Trauma and its aftermath for commercially sexually exploited women as told by front-line service providers. *Issues in Mental Health Nursing*, 34(2), 75–81.

Home Affairs Committee, 2016. *Conclusions and Recommendations*. London: HMSO. Available at: https://publications.parliament.uk/pa/cm201617/cmselect/cmhaff/26/2609.htm [accessed 11 March 2022].

Home Office, 2008. *Tackling the Demand for Prostitution: A Review*. London: Home Office. Available at: http://webarchive.nationalarchives.gov.uk/20100418065544/http:/homeoffice.gov.uk/documents/tackling-demand2835.pdf?view=Binary [accessed 18 May 2021].

Hope, T. and Walters, R., 2008. *Critical Thinking about the Uses of Research*. Kings College, London: Centre for Crime and Justice Studies. Available at: https://www.crimeandjustice.org.uk/publications/critical-thinking-about-uses-research [accessed 1 July 2021].

Hubbard, P., 2009. Opposing striptopia: The embattled spaces of adult entertainment. *Sexualities*, 12(6), 721–745.

Hubbard, P. and Colosi, R., 2015. Respectability, morality and disgust in the night-time economy: Exploring reactions to 'lap dance' clubs in England and Wales. *The Sociological Review*, 63(4), 782–800.

Huff, A.D., 2011. Buying the girlfriend experience: An exploration of the consumption experiences of male customers of escorts. In: R. Ahluwalia, T.L. Chartrand and R.K. Ratner (eds), *Advances in Consumer Research Volume 39*. Duluth: Association for Consumer Research, pp 447–448.

Hughes, R., Kinder, A. and Cooper, C., 2012. *International Handbook of Workplace Trauma Support*. Chichester and Malden, MA: Wiley-Blackwell.

Hull Lighthouse Project, 2017. *An Untold Story: Experiences of Life and Street Prostitution in Hull*. Hull: Hull Lighthouse Project.

Jeffreys, S., 1997. *The Idea of Prostitution*, 1st edition. Melbourne: Spinifex Press.

Joseph, L.J. and Black, P., 2012. Who's the man? Fragile masculinities, consumer masculinities, and the profiles of sex work clients. *Men and Masculinities*, 15(5), 486–506.

Kassirer, K., 2019. *A Whore's Manifesto: An Anthology of Writing and Artwork by Sex Workers*. Portland: Thorntree Press.

Katsulis, Y., 2010. Living like a king: Conspicuous consumption, virtual communities, and the social construction of paid sexual encounters by U.S. sex tourists. *Men and Masculinities*, 13(2), 210–230.

Kenney, S., 2012. Full disclosure: The modern sex worker memoir. *Creative Nonfiction*, 45(20120701), 62–64. Available at: https://www-jstor-org.bris.idm.oclc.org/stable/44364931 [accessed 11 March 2022].

Kingston, S., Hammond, N. and Redman, S., 2020. Transformational sexualities: Motivations of women who pay for sexual services. *Sexualities*, 24(4), 527–548. https://doi.org/10.1177/1363460720904646

Lincoln, Y.S. and Guba, E.G., 1985. *Naturalistic Inquiry*. Beverly Hills: SAGE Publications.

Lindemann, D., 2011. BDSM as therapy? *Sexualities*, 14(2), 151–172.

Logan, T., 2017. Male sex work: Antiquity to online. In: T. Logan, *Economics, Sexuality and Male Sex Work*. Cambridge: Cambridge University Press, Ch. 1.

Ma, P., Chan, Z.C.Y. and Loke, A.Y., 2018. Conflicting identities between sex workers and motherhood: A systematic review. *Women & Health*, 59(3), 534–557.

Månsson, S.A., 2005. Men's Practices in Prostitution and their Implications for Social Work. In: S.A. Månsson and C. Proveyer Cervantes (eds), *Social Work in Cuba and Sweden: Achievements and Prospects*. Department of Social Work, Göteborg University, 267–279.

Mayring, P., 2000. Qualitative content analysis. *Forum: Qualitative Social Research*, 1(2), 1–20.

Mazzei, I., 2019. *Camgirl*. Los Angeles: Rare Bird Books.

McChesney, K. and Aldridge, J., 2019. Weaving an interpretivist stance throughout mixed methods research. *International Journal of Research & Method in Education*, 42(3), 225–238.

McCoyd, J.L.M. and Shdaimah, C.S., 2007. Revisiting the Benefits Debate: Does Qualitative Social Work Research Produce Salubrious Effects? *Social Work*, 52(4), 40–349.

McNeill, M. 2012. Whorearchy. *The Honest Courtesan*, 10 May. Available at: https://maggiemcneill.wordpress.com/2012/05/10/whorearchy/ [accessed 15 July 2021].

Milrod, C. and Monto, M.A., 2012. The hobbyist and the girlfriend experience: Behaviors and preferences of male customers of internet sexual service providers. *Deviant Behavior*, 33(10), 792–810.

Minichiello, V. and Scott, J.G., eds, 2014. *Male Sex Work and Society*. New York: Harrington Park Press.

Monto, M. and Milrod, C., 2020. Perceptions of provider power among sex buyers. *Sexualities*, 23(4), 630–644.

Moran, R., 2015. *Paid for: My Journey Through Prostitution*. New York: W. W. Norton & Company.

Morris, M., 2018. *Incidental Sex Work: Casual and Commercial Encounters in Queer Digital Spaces*. PhD thesis, Durham University.

Morris, M., 2021. The limits of labelling: Incidental sex work among gay, bisexual, and queer young men on social media. *Sexualities Research and Social Policy*. https://doi.org/10.1007/s13178-021-00603-9

Morse, J.M., 2015. Critical analysis of strategies for determining rigor in qualitative inquiry. *Qualitative Health Research*, 25, 1212–1222.

Mulvihill, N., 2019. Is it time to drop the term 'prostitution' from policy discourse? *Journal of Gender-Based Violence*, 3(3), 385–393.

Mulvihill, N. and Large, J., 2019. Consuming authenticity: Pleasure, benefit and harm in 'transactional intimacy' and 'slum tourism'. *Justice, Power and Resistance*, 3(2), 103–124.

Mulvihill, N., Hart, A., Northmore, S., Wolff, D. and Pratt, J., 2011. *Models of Partnership Working in University: Community Engagement*. Brighton: Community University Partnership Programme (Cupp). Available at: http://www.coastalcommunities.org.uk/briefing%20papers/Paper_2vgreen.pdf

National Survey of Sexual Attitudes and Lifestyles, 1990-to date. Project managed by University College London (UCL), the London School of Hygiene & Tropical Medicine (LSHTM), the University of Glasgow and NatCen Social Research (NatCen). Available at: https://www.natsal.ac.uk/ [Accessed on 9 March 2022].

National Ugly Mugs (NUM) and Femmedaemonium, 2020. *The Source Zine: Voices from Sex Workers of Colour*. Issue #001. Available at: https://www.femmedeamon.com/the-source [accessed 11 March 2022].

Nayar, K.I., 2017. Sweetening the deal: Dating for compensation in the digital age. *Journal of Gender Studies*, 26(3), 335–346.

Nuttbrock, L.A. and Bockting, W.O., 2018. *Transgender Sex Work and Society*. New York: Harrington Park Press.

O'Connell Davidson, J., 1998. *Prostitution, Power and Freedom*. Oxford and Cambridge: Polity Press.

O'Kelly, S., 2012. *Paying for It: How Turning Tricks Paid the Mortgage, Kept the Kids in Trainers and Gave Me My Life Back*. London: Penguin Books.

Oliveira, E., 2016. Empowering, invasive or a little bit of both? A reflection on the use of visual and narrative methods in research with migrant sex workers in South Africa. *Visual Studies*, 31(3), 260–278.

O'Neill, M., 1996. Researching prostitution and violence: Towards a feminist praxis. In: M. Hester, L. Radford and L. Kelly (eds), *Researching Male Violence*. Milton Keynes: Open University Press, pp 130–147.

Orchard, T., Vale, J., Macphail, S., Wender, C. and Oiamo, T., 2016. "You just have to be smart": Spatial practices and subjectivity among women in sex work. *Gender, Place & Culture*, 26(11), 1572–1585.

Orchard, T., Salter, K., Bunch, M. and Benoit, C., 2020. Money, agency, and self-care among cisgender and trans people in sex work. *Social Sciences*, 10(6). https://www.mdpi.com/2076-0760/10/1/6 [accessed 11 March 2022].

Personal Narratives Group, 1989. *Interpreting Women's Lives: Feminist Theory and Personal Narratives*. Bloomington: Indiana University Press.

Petro, M., Herman, A., Saini, A., Chase, M., Vera, V., Wright, D., Essence Revealed, Ryley, J., Kenney, K., and Lovely Brown, 2014. *Prose and Lore: Issue 1: Memoir Stories About Sex Work*. New York: Red Umbrella Project.

Phoenix, J., 1999. *Making Sense of Prostitution*. London: Palgrave Macmillan.

Pilcher, K., 2012a. Dancing for women: Subverting heteronormativity in a lesbian erotic dance space? *Sexualities*, 15(5–6), 521–537.

Pilcher, K., 2012b. A 'sexy space' for women? Heterosexual women's experiences of a male strip show venue. In: J. Caudwell and K. Browne (eds), *Sexualities, Spaces and Leisure Studies*. London: Routledge, pp 119–138.

Pilcher, K., 2017. *Erotic Performance and Spectatorship: New Frontiers in Erotic Dance*. London: Routledge.

Pitcher, J., 2015. Sex work and modes of self-employment in the informal economy: Diverse business practices and constraints to effective working. *Social Policy and Society*, 14(1), 113–123.

Presser, L., 2005. Negotiating power and narrative in research: Implications for feminist methodology. *Signs: Journal of Women in Culture and Society*, 30(4), 2067–2090.

Ratislavová, K. and Ratislav, J., 2014. Asynchronous email interview as a qualitative research method in the humanities. *Human Affairs*, 24(4), 452–460.

Report of the Committee on Homosexual Offences and Prostitution, 1957. [Wolfenden Committee] (Cmnd. 247). London: HMSO.

Riessman, C.K., 1993. *Narrative Analysis*. Newbury Park: SAGE Publications.

Ritchie, J. and Spencer, L., 2002. Qualitative Data Analysis for Applied Policy Research. In: A.M. Huberman and M.B. Miles (eds), *The Qualitative Researcher's Companion*. London: SAGE Publications, 305–329.

Sagar, T., Jones, D., Croxall, J., Tyrie, J. & Chimba, M., 2011. *Locating Female Black and Minority Ethnic Off Street Sex Workers in Cardiff*. Swansea: Swansea University.

Sagar, T., Jones, D., Symons, K. and Bowring, J., 2015. *The Student Sex Work Project: Research Summary*. Available at: http://www.thestudentsexwork project.co.uk/wp-content/uploads/2015/03/TSSWP-Research-Summ ary-English.pdf [accessed 9 March 2022].

Sagar, T., Jones, D., Symons, K., Tyrie, J. and Roberts, R. 2016. Student involvement in the UK sex industry: Motivations and experiences. *The British Journal of Sociology*, 67(4), 697–718.

Samudzi, Z., 2017. *Thematic Network Analysis and Feminist Methodologies: Analyzing Narratives of Agency and Exclusion of Transgender Women in Sex Work*. SAGE Research Methods. Available at: https://meth ods-sagepub-com.bris.idm.oclc.org/case/thematic-network-analysis-femin ist-methodologies-transgender-women-sex [accessed 12 July 2021].

Sanders, T., 2007. Becoming an ex-sex worker: Making transitions out of a deviant career. *Feminist Criminology*, 2(1), 74–95.

Sanders, T., 2008. *Paying for Pleasure: Men who Buy Sex*. Cullompton: Willan.

Sanders, T. and Hardy, K., 2012. Devalued, deskilled and diversified: Explaining the proliferation of the strip industry in the UK. *The British Journal of Sociology*, 63(3), 513–532.

Sanders, T., Scoular, J., Campbell, R., Pitcher, J. and Cunningham, S., 2017. *Internet Sex Work: Beyond the Gaze*. London: Palgrave Macmillan.

Sanders, T., O'Neill, M. and Pitcher, J., 2018. *Prostitution: Sex Work, Policy & Politics*. London: SAGE Publications.

Sanders, T., Pitcher, J., Scoular, J., Campbell, R. and Cunningham, S., 2021. Male independent sex workers in the digital age: Online male escorting in the United Kingdom. In: J.G. Scott, C. Grov and V. Minichiello (eds), *The Routledge Handbook of Male Sex Work, Culture, and Society*. Abingdon: Routledge, pp 272–286.

Schwandt, T.A., 1998. Constructivist, interpretivist approaches to human inquiry. In: N.K. Denzin and Y.S. Lincoln (eds), *The Landscape of Qualitative Research: Theories and Issues*. Thousand Oaks: SAGE Publications, pp 221–259.

Scott, J., Hunter, J., Hunter, V. and Ragusa A., 2006. Sex outside the city: Sex work in rural and regional New South Wales. *Rural Society*, 16(2), 151–167.

Sex Worker Advocacy and Worker Resistance Movement, 2019. *Shadow Report to CEDAW*. Available at: https://tbinternet.ohchr.org/Treaties/CEDAW/Shared%20Documents/GBR/INT_CEDAW_CSS_GBR_3365 8_E.docx [accessed 12 July 2021].

Smith, J.A., 1994. Towards reflexive practice: Engaging participants as co-researchers or co-analysts in psychological inquiry. *Community & Applied Social Psychology*, 4(4), 253–260.

Smith, M. and Mac, J., 2020. *Revolting Prostitutes: The Fight for Sex Workers' Rights*. London: Verso

Soothill, K. and Sanders, T., 2005. The geographical mobility, preferences and pleasures of prolific punters: A demonstration study of the activities of prostitutes' clients. *Sociological Research Online*, 10(1), 17–30.

Spanger, M., 2011. Human trafficking as a lever for feminist voices? Transformations of the Danish policy field of prostitution. *Critical Social Policy*, 31(4), 517–539.

Sterry, D.H. and Martin, R.J., 2009. *Hos, Hookers, Call Girls, and Rent Boys: Professionals Writing on Life, Love, Money, and Sex*. Berkeley, CA: Soft Skull Press.

Sterry, D.H. and Martin, R.J., 2013. *Johns, Marks, Tricks and Chickenhawks: Professionals & Their Clients Writing about Each Other*. Berkeley, CA: Soft Skull Press.

Stevens v Christy [1987] Cr. App. R. 249, DC.

Tade, O. and Adekoya, A.J., 2012. Transactional sex and the 'aristo' phenomenon in Nigerian universities. *Human Affairs*, 22(2), 239–255.

Tankard Reist, M., and Norma, C., eds, 2016. *Prostitution Narratives: Stories of Survival in Sex Trade*. Melbourne: Spinifex Press.

Tewksbury, R.A. and Lapsey, D., 2017. Male escorts' construction of the boyfriend experience: How escorts please their clients. *International Journal of Sexual Health*, 29(4), 292–302.

Thiara, R. and Roy, S., 2020. *Reclaiming Voice: Minoritised Women and Sexual Violence: Key Findings*. London: Imkaan. Available at: https://www.imkaan.org.uk/resources [accessed 11 March 2022].

Thomas, D.R., 2017. Feedback from research participants: Are member checks useful in qualitative research?, *Qualitative Research in Psychology*, 14(1), 23–41.

Thouin-Savard, M.I., 2019. Erotic mindfulness: A core educational and therapeutic strategy in somatic sexology practices. *The International Journal of Transpersonal Studies*, 38(1), 203–219.

Tracy, S.J., 2010. Qualitative quality: Eight 'big-tent' criteria for excellent qualitative research. *Qualitative Inquiry*, 16(10), 837–851.

Vandepitte, J., Lyerla, R., Dallabetta, G., Crabbé, F., Alary, M. and Buvé, A., 2006. Estimates of the number of female sex workers in different regions of the world. *Sexually Transmitted Infections*, 82(Suppl 3): iii18–iii25.

Van Schuylenbergh, J., Motmans, J. and Coene, G., 2018. Transgender and non-binary persons and sexual risk: A critical review of 10 years of research from a feminist intersectional perspective. *Critical Social Policy*, 38(1), 121–142.

Ward, H., Mercer, C.H., Wellings, K., Fenton, K.A., Erens, B., Copas, A.J. and Johnson, A.M., 2005. Who pays for sex? An analysis of the increasing prevalence of female commercial sex contacts among men in Britain. *Sexually Transmitted Infections*, 81(6), 467–471.

Watt, N., 2008. Labour conference: Total ban for sex soliciting and kerb-crawling. *Guardian Online*, 22 September. Available at: http://www.guard ian.co.uk/politics/2008/sep/22/labourconference.labour1 [accessed 18 May 2021].

Weeks, J., 1981. *Sex, Politics and Society*. London: Longman.

Wetherell, M., Taylor, S. and Yates, S.J., 2005. *Discourse, Theory and Practice: A Reader*. London: SAGE Publications.

Whowell, M., 2010. Male Sex Work: Exploring Regulation in England and Wales. *Journal of Law and Society*, 37(1), 125–144.

Winter v Woolfe [1931] KB 549.

Women and Equalities Committee, 2018. *Sexual Harassment of Women and Girls in Public Places. Sixth Report of Session 2017–2019.* [HC 701] London: House of Commons. Available at: https://publications.parliam ent.uk/pa/cm201719/cmselect/cmwomeq/701/701.pdf [accessed 15 July 2021].

Index

References to figures appear in *italic* type;
those in **bold** type refer to tables.

www.ingramcontent.com/pod-product-compliance
Lightning Source LLC
Chambersburg PA
CBHW070637030426
42337CB00020B/4053